Content

Introduction - The Journey to Stress-Free High Achievement	03
Chapter 1 - The Myth of Busy Success	03
Chapter 2 - Rethinking Stress in Success	05
Chapter 3 - Productivity Beyond Time Constraints	06
Chapter 4 - The Tool Trap: Quality Over Quantity	10
Chapter 5 - Managing Self, Not Time	13
Chapter 6 - Comfort, Procrastination and Their Discontents	13
Chapter 7 - Old Versus New Productivity Paradigms	13
Chapter 8 - Master of Self for Peak Performance	13
Chapter 9 - Leadership and Relationships: The Core of Success	13
Chapter 10 - Integrating Purpose and Principles for a High Achieving Life	13
Conclusion - Your Path Forward as a Stress-Free High Achiever	13

Introduction

"The path to stress-free high achievement begins with the courage to redefine success on your own terms."

Damian Tang

INTRODUCTION

The Journey to Stress-Free High Achievement

In the vibrant mosaic of professional and personal development, ambition is often intertwined with a relentless pursuit of excellence, shadowed by the omnipresent specter of stress. My journey, evolving from the structured discipline of public service to the innovative expanse of entrepreneurship, embodies the essence of this book: a testament to the transformative power of redefining success. I am Damian Tang, a landscape architect turned pioneering entrepreneur, whose path has illuminated the way for those seeking not just to achieve but to do so with balance, purpose, and joy. "Stress-Free High Achievers" invites aspiring leaders and successful individuals to challenge the conventional equation of success with perpetual busyness, advocating instead for a paradigm where strategic focus, prioritisation, and inner harmony are the keystones of true achievement.

— Damian

My professional narrative, rooted in a comprehensive educational background from the University of Melbourne, enriched with specialized knowledge in Circular Economy and Sustainability Strategies from the University of Cambridge Judge Business School, has been a relentless quest for excellence. From impactful roles within National Parks Board, Singapore to leadership positions in prestigious landscape architecture organisations, and eventually to spearheading innovative neurodesign ventures like URDX Studio and circular economy under Circular Cities Worldwide Pte Ltd and few other partner ventures and investment, my journey is one of continuous evolution and unwavering commitment to sustainable innovation.

Yet, amidst this whirlwind of accomplishments, a profound realisation emerged: the glorification of busyness, often mistaken for productivity, was a mirage leading away from true fulfillment and impact. This epiphany, born from introspection, transformative coaching and episodes of trauma therapy, marked a pivotal shift in my understanding of success—from a state of constant activity to one of meaningful engagement and stress-free high performance.

Leading the Charge Towards Sustainable Success

Currently, as the Chairman of the Circular Cities Summit and Director-General of Circular Cities Network, representing eight global organisations, my role transcends personal achievements to influence the global narrative on urban sustainability. This position not only underscores the international acknowledgment of my endeavors but also epitomises my dedication to championing a sustainable future through collaborative innovation and strategic leadership.

May This Book Be Your Compass

"Stress-Free High Achievers" is not merely a recount of my professional odyssey; it's a guide for those at the nexus of ambition and well-being. It's for the visionary leaders, the relentless innovators, the passionate dreamers, and the determined doers who seek to redefine success beyond the confines of busyness. Whether you're embarking on your career journey, leading a team towards groundbreaking milestones, or pioneering your own entrepreneurial venture, this book offers insights and strategies to achieve excellence without the shadow of stress.

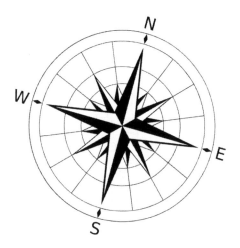

Embark on this transformative exploration to redefine success. This book sets the stage for a journey measured not by the ticking clock but by the depth of our contributions, the impact of our work, and the harmony within our lives. Welcome to the path of the stress-free high achiever, where success is not a race against time but a journey toward growth, innovation, leadership, and inner peace. This book is for you—the ambitious soul seeking to make a significant mark on the world while maintaining a serene, balanced, and fulfilling existence.

Chapter 1

"Busy is not a badge of honour; it's a distraction from true achievement."

Damian Tang

CHAPTER ONE

The Myth of Busy Success

In today's fast-paced world, the concept of "busy" has become synonymous with success. The busier you are, the more successful you must be—or so the myth goes. This chapter is an invitation to challenge this pervasive belief and to redefine what true success looks like. It draws on my own journey, once marked by a ceaseless flurry of projects, voluntary work, and an underlying pride in my constant state of busyness. It's a story of awakening to the realisation that perpetual busyness does not inherently equate to meaningful success or fulfilment.

The Allure of Busyness

For years, my life was a testament to the glorification of busy. Each day was a marathon of tasks, meetings, and commitments, a juggling act performed under the banner of productivity. I wore my busyness like a badge of honour, believing it was a tangible sign of my dedication, importance, and, ultimately, my success. However, beneath the surface of this bustling activity lay a troubling reality: a cycle of endless tasks that, while keeping me busy, rarely brought me closer to my true goals or personal fulfillment.

The Awakening

The turning point came when I paused to reflect on the nature of my so-called productivity. It was also a time when my relationships with people, including my marriage broke down, my health suffered, and I lost my drive to go to work every single day. Amidst the chaos of back-to-back commitments, I realised that my busyness was a hollow pursuit. It was a shield against the deeper questions of purpose, impact, and satisfaction. This revelation was uncomfortable but necessary, leading me to question the very foundations of what I considered success.

Rethinking Success: Beyond the Busy Veil

The journey from recognising the futility of constant busyness to redefining success was transformative. It involved understanding that strategic focus and prioritising tasks are far more valuable than the mere act of being busy. The pitfalls of equating busyness with productivity became glaringly obvious, guiding me towards a more intentional and purpose-driven approach to work and life.

Takeaways for a New Paradigm

- Abandon the 'Busy' Badge: It's time to strip 'busyness' of its unwarranted prestige. Let's remove "busy" from our vocabulary, especially when it serves as a mask for self-pity or a plea for empathy rather than a statement of meaningful engagement.

- Reframe 'Busy' with Purpose: If we choose to use the word 'busy,' let it be in contexts that reflect success, fulfillment, and joy. "I am busy" should precede statements of positive outcomes and purposeful actions, such as, "I am busy closing a deal that will significantly advance my career," or "I am busy nurturing valuable moments with my loved ones."

- Keep Purpose and Goals in Sight: Changing the context of 'busy' from a negative to a positive helps maintain a clear focus on our true purposes and goals. It acts as a litmus test for our activities: if we can't frame our busyness in terms that align with our objectives and aspirations, perhaps it's time to reconsider how we spend our time.

This first chapter is not merely an introduction to debunking the myth of busy success; it's an invitation to embark on a journey of self-discovery and redefine success on your terms, and with a purpose. As we progress through this book, we'll explore strategies for living and working with intention, ensuring that our actions lead us not just to the appearance of success, but to its most authentic and fulfilling expression.

Let's step away from the shadow of busyness and into the light of purposeful achievement.

Chapter 2

"True productivity transcends the limitations of time; it's about the quality of your actions, not the quantity of hours worked."

Damian Tang

CHAPTER TWO

Rethinking Stress in Success

In the relentless pursuit of success, stress often emerges as an uninvited yet seemingly inseparable companion. Our societal narrative has long painted stress as the inevitable price of achievement, a notion deeply ingrained in the professional psyche. Yet, what if we've been approaching it all wrong? This chapter is inspired by my own journey through the highs and lows of professional advancement, where the accolades and promotions came at a steep cost to my personal relationships and well-being. It's a story not uncommon in the cutthroat realms of ambition, but it's also a narrative ripe for change.

Imagine, if you will, the process of forging steel. Under intense heat and pressure, raw iron transforms into something stronger, more resilient. Society often likens stress to this process—a necessary force in shaping successful individuals. However, this analogy misses a crucial aspect: even steel has its breaking point when subjected to unrelenting stress. In my quest for professional recognition, I became that piece of steel, unaware that the very process I thought was making me stronger was actually pushing me to the brink of my own resilience.

The revelation came not with more accolades or achievements, but with an understanding of the delicate dance between stress and success. I learned that stress, much like fire in the forge, needs to be managed with care to not consume entirely. This chapter delves into redefining our relationship with stress, challenging the entrenched belief that it is an indispensable aspect of success. It's about changing the language we use when we face stress, recognizing that the words we choose can shape our experience and resilience.

Here, I share strategies that allowed me to manage stress and maintain peak performance without sacrificing my well-being. From personal anecdotes to scientific insights, this chapter offers a holistic approach to understanding how our bodies and minds interact with stress. It's an invitation to rethink stress in the context of success, recognising that the path to our greatest achievements does not have to be paved with relentless pressure and strain.

This journey is about more than just managing stress; it's about transforming our perception of what it means to be successful. By redefining our relationship with stress, we can pursue our ambitions with vigor, supported by a foundation of well-being and resilience. Welcome to a new chapter in your path to success—one where stress is no longer a foe to battle but a force to be understood and mastered.

What is your relationship with stress?

Navigating the Landscape of Stress

In life's journey, stress is an unavoidable companion, manifesting as both an emotional state and a physical sensation. Understanding stress, how we inadvertently nourish it, and reshaping our relationship with it are vital steps toward navigating its challenges.

Understanding Stress

1. Stress is a complex phenomenon involving both psychological and physiological components. It arises not only from emotional distress but also triggers a cascade of physical responses within the body.

2. Emotionally, stress can manifest as feelings of anxiety, unease, or tension. These sensations often accompany thoughts of impending danger or overwhelm.

3. Physiologically, stress activates the body's "fight or flight" response, leading to increased heart rate, elevated blood pressure, and heightened muscle tension. These changes prepare the body to react quickly to perceived threats.

Feeding the Beast:

1. Stress is perpetuated by certain behaviors that unwittingly fuel its intensity and duration. These behaviors include:

- Worrying excessively about potential outcomes or future events, which keeps the mind in a state of apprehension and amplifies stress levels.

- Procrastinating on tasks or responsibilities, leading to a buildup of pressure and exacerbating feelings of stress as deadlines loom closer.

- Overcommitting oneself to tasks, obligations, or responsibilities, spreading thin resources and time, and leaving little room for relaxation or self-care.

2. The language we use to describe and interpret stress can significantly shape our experience of it. Positive framing and constructive self-talk can help mitigate stress, while negative or catastrophic language may intensify feelings of anxiety and overwhelm.

3. By becoming aware of how we speak about stress and actively choosing more empowering and affirming language, we can exert greater control over its impact on our mental and emotional well-being.

A New Dialogue

The language we use in our inner dialogue and outward expressions has the power to shape our reality. By consciously choosing words that empower rather than diminish, we can transform our relationship with stress. Instead of viewing tasks as burdens, we can see them as opportunities for growth or learning. This shift not only changes our internal narrative but also influences our emotional and physiological responses to stress.

- Words are powerful and shape our reality and mindset.
- Instead of saying, "I am stressed," acknowledge the situation more objectively: "I have quite a lot of tasks to deliver. And I just need to deal with it, one at a time."

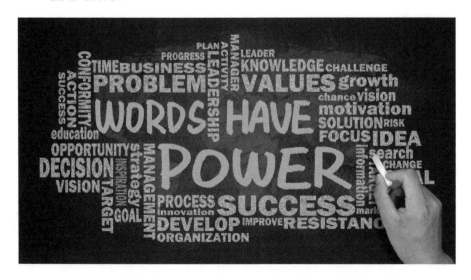

Words and Phrases to Avoid and Their Alternatives

1. Avoid: "I'm swamped."
   Alternative: "My schedule is full, but I'm organizing my priorities."

2. Avoid: "This is a nightmare."
   Alternative: "This situation is challenging, but I'm seeking solutions."

3. Avoid: "I have no choice."
   Alternative: "I have a few options to consider."

4. Avoid: "I'm at my limit."
   Alternative: "I need to take a moment to reassess my workload."

5. Avoid: "I'll never finish on time."
   Alternative: "I'm focusing on making consistent progress."

6. Avoid: "This has to be perfect."
   Alternative: "I aim for excellence but accept that perfection is unattainable."

7. Avoid: "I should be able to handle this."
   Alternative: "I'm doing my best and learning as I go."

8. Avoid: "It's all going wrong."
   Alternative: "There are obstacles, but also opportunities for correction."

9. Avoid: "I'm drowning in this."
   Alternative: "I'm facing a lot, but I'm finding ways to navigate through."

10. Avoid: "I'm stuck."
    Alternative: "I'm looking for a new perspective to move forward."

11. Avoid: "I'm stressed."
    Alternative: "I'm facing some challenges, but I'm working through them."

12. Avoid: "I can't handle this."
    Alternative: "This is tough, but I'm finding ways to cope."

13. Avoid: "This is impossible."
 Alternative: "This requires some creative problem-solving."

14. Avoid: "I'm overwhelmed."
 Alternative: "I have a lot on my plate, and I'm prioritizing my tasks."

Embracing Action Over Identity
- Change in dialogue leads to a shift in mindset from overwhelm to action.
- Prioritise tasks, engage in self-care, and build resilience through manageable challenges.

The Journey Forward

- Transform your relationship with stress by managing emotions, willpower, and adopting a more positive dialogue.

- View stress as a series of challenges rather than a defining part of your identity.

Strategies for a Balanced Life

Adopting strategies that foster emotional resilience, conserve willpower, and promote awareness can significantly alter our stress landscape.

Mindfulness and Meditation:
These practices offer a refuge from the storm of stress, creating space for calmness and clarity. They teach us to observe our thoughts and feelings without judgment, providing a foundation for more mindful responses to stress.

Physical Activity:
Regular exercise is a proven stress reliever. It enhances our mood, clears our mind, and builds physical resilience, making us less susceptible to the negative impacts of stress.

Healthy Connections:
Cultivating supportive relationships provides emotional nourishment, reducing feelings of isolation and overwhelm. Sharing our experiences and seeking support can lighten our load and introduce new perspectives.

Restorative Sleep:
Prioritising quality sleep is essential for replenishing our energy, healing our bodies, and maintaining cognitive function. Establishing a restful bedtime routine can enhance sleep quality and resilience to stress.

Key Takeaway

- The emotional journey through stress is about changing how we interact with it.

- By understanding stress and employing strategic language changes, we can navigate life's challenges with resilience and awareness.

By adopting this approach, we not only manage stress more effectively but also pave the way for a balanced and fulfilling life. The goal is to learn from our encounters with stress, using them as opportunities for growth and personal development.

Chapter 3

"True productivity transcends the limitations of time; it's about the quality of your actions, not the quantity of hours worked."

Damian Tang

CHAPTER THREE

Productivity Beyond Time Constraints

In a world where the ticking clock governs our lives, we often fall into the trap of equating productivity with the ability to do more in less time. This chapter aims to dismantle that misconception, advocating for a focus on quality, effectiveness, and the establishment of sustainable working patterns. Through my own experiences and the wisdom gleaned from transformative insights, I've learned that true productivity is not about racing against time but about making every moment count in a meaningful way.

My Journey: From Exhaustion to Enlightenment

When I took on the position of the President of the Singapore Institute of Landscape Architects and the Design Director in the Public Service in 2010, I faced the colossal challenge of excelling in dual roles. My days were a blur of commitments, with the daunting task of delivering quality work in both capacities. Driven by a resolve to succeed, I embarked on a quest to maximise my productivity, equating it with speed and volume of work completed.

This approach, however, led me down a path of compromised quality and personal exhaustion. The pursuit of doing more in less time was unsustainable, leaving me fatigued and my work, less impactful. It was a cycle of diminishing returns, where the more I pushed for efficiency, the more the essence of my work and well-being eroded.

An awakening point came from a transformative coaching program. A coach shared an analogy that forever altered my perspective on productivity:

"Consider a gardener tending to a garden. Rushing to plant, water, and prune without attention to the needs of each plant leads to a neglected, unthriving garden. However, a gardener who takes time to understand and care for each plant individually will see a garden flourish. Productivity, like gardening, requires nurturing and patience more than it does haste."

This insight illuminated the importance of focusing on effectiveness rather than mere efficiency. It was a profound lesson in understanding that true productivity lies in the quality and impact of our work, not just the speed of task completion.

The Misconception of Multitasking

Drawing from Daniel J. Levitin's "The Organized Mind", I delved into the science of how our brains process information. Levitin's research highlights the fallacy of multitasking - rather than increasing productivity, overloading the brain with tasks leads to decreased effectiveness. The brain, when forced to juggle multiple tasks, loses its ability to focus deeply, resulting in a superficial engagement with work that lacks depth and quality.

Integration of this understanding into my daily routines involved a conscious effort to prioritise tasks and focus on one at a time. This single-tasking approach allowed for deeper immersion and creativity, leading to outcomes that were not only more satisfying but also of significantly higher quality. It was at this juncture in my journey that my fascination with neuroscience and its impact on human behavior, particularly in relation to our interaction with spatial environments and activities, was piqued. Driven by an insatiable curiosity for neuroarchitecture, I found myself delving deeper into research during my free time. This exploration not only enriched my understanding but also directly informed my design practices. Indeed, it was this continuous quest for knowledge that inspired the writing of this book, as I sought to share insights gleaned from neuroscience and its application in my professional design endeavors.

For further exploration, I invite you to visit my website at www.urdxstudio.com.

But for now, let us return to the practical implications of this science and research. Let's delve into a checklist that can serve as a valuable tool in leveraging this understanding to enhance your own endeavors.

Your Daily Checklist:
1. Identify Priorities: Start each day by identifying the tasks that truly matter.
2. Set Clear Goals: Define specific and achievable objectives for each task.
3. Single-Tasking: Embrace the power of focusing on one task at a time.
4. Minimise Distractions: Create a conducive environment by eliminating potential distractions.
5. Time Blocking: Allocate dedicated time slots for each task to maintain focus.
6. Practice Mindfulness: Cultivate present-moment awareness to stay fully engaged.
7. Take Breaks: Incorporate short breaks to recharge and maintain mental clarity.
8. Reflect and Adjust: Regularly evaluate your productivity and adapt your approach as needed.
9. Celebrate Progress: Acknowledge your achievements and milestones along the way.
10. Seek Support: Don't hesitate to reach out for assistance or guidance when needed.

With these tools at our disposal, it would be easier to embark on a journey toward greater productivity, creativity, and fulfilment.

Takeaways for Sustainable Productivity

- Quality Over Quantity: True productivity is measured not by the volume of tasks completed but by the impact and quality of the work produced.

- Effectiveness Over Efficiency: While efficiency is about doing things quickly, effectiveness is about doing the right things well. Balancing the two is key to sustainable productivity.

- The Power of Single-Tasking: In an age of information overload, focusing on one task at a time enhances our ability to work creatively and effectively.

- Nurturing Productivity: Like the gardener's careful attention to each plant, nurturing our tasks with mindfulness and patience yields the richest results.

This chapter is a testament to the transformative power of redefining productivity. By shifting our focus from the clock to the content of our work,

we can achieve a level of productivity that is not only sustainable but also deeply fulfilling. The journey from exhaustion to enlightenment is a path that leads us to discover that within the constraints of time lies the boundless potential for creativity, impact, and personal growth.

Chapter 4

"In the pursuit of productivity, it's not the abundance of tools that matters, but the mastery of those that truly serve your purpose."

Damian Tang

CHAPTER FOUR

The Tool Trap: Quality Over Quantity

In the journey from the tactile world of landscape architecture to the strategic realm of entrepreneurship, I've learned that the true power lies not in the quantity of tools at one's disposal, but in the careful selection and mastery of a few that truly enhance productivity and creativity. This evolution in my approach to tools reflects a universal principle that transcends sectors, emphasising the need for quality over quantity. To make this principle contextual and applicable for readers across different sectors, here are some easy-to-apply tools and a step-by-step guide to streamline your toolset effectively.

From Designer to Entrepreneur: A Shift in Toolset

As I reflect on the journey from my humble beginnings in landscape architecture to my current role as an entrepreneur, I am reminded of the evolution of my toolkit. In those early days, my arsenal was stocked with the tangible implements of my trade: drafting software humming on my computer, sketching pencils poised for creation, and a plethora of paper types awaiting my ideas. These tools were the conduits through which my creativity flowed, promising to transform concepts into tangible realities.

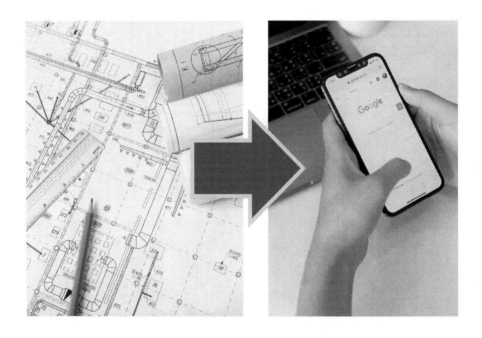

Yet, as my career trajectory veered towards management and entrepreneurship, I found myself grappling with an unexpected dilemma: the burden of abundance. My once-beloved array of tools had become cumbersome, both physically and mentally. The clutter that once fueled my creativity now stifled it, leading to decision fatigue and a sense of overwhelm. I realised that in order to thrive in this new landscape, I needed to undergo a radical transformation—a shift in my toolset that prioritised efficiency, clarity, and focus.

This pivotal realisation marked the beginning of a deliberate process of curation and refinement. Gone were the days of accumulating tools for the sake of variety; instead, I embraced the ethos of minimalism, paring down my toolkit to only the essentials. Quality replaced quantity as the guiding principle, with each tool meticulously selected to serve a specific purpose and enhance productivity.

In place of the cluttered chaos of my past, I cultivated a workspace characterised by simplicity and intentionality. Digital tools became my allies, seamlessly integrating into my workflow to streamline processes and eliminate unnecessary friction. Project management software replaced stacks of paper, providing a centralised hub for collaboration and organization. Cloud-based platforms facilitated seamless communication and file sharing, breaking down barriers and enabling remote collaboration across geographical boundaries.

Yet, this transformation was not confined to the physical realm; it permeated every aspect of my professional practice. Embracing the principles of mindfulness and self-awareness, I honed my ability to discern between noise and signal, prioritising tasks that aligned with my overarching goals and values. The mental clarity that ensued allowed me to channel my energy into meaningful pursuits, fostering innovation and driving growth.

Today, as I navigate the dynamic landscape of entrepreneurship, I am grateful for the lessons learned from this transformative journey. My streamlined toolset serves not only as a catalyst for productivity but also as a reflection of my evolving mindset—a testament to the power of intentionality and focus in achieving success. As I continue to chart new territories and embrace new challenges, I do so with a newfound appreciation for the profound impact of simplicity in unleashing creativity and unlocking potential.

Streamlining for Efficiency and Creativity

Transitioning from the hands-on world of design to the strategic realm of entrepreneurship necessitated a fundamental reevaluation of my toolkit. With new roles, responsibilities, and aspirations on the horizon, I embarked on a journey to align my tools with the demands of this dynamic landscape. Here's how my approach evolved, along with practical tips for streamlining efficiency and fostering creativity:

In Management:
- **Project Management Tools**:
Embracing leadership roles underscored the critical importance of efficient project management. I sought out robust project management software, such as Asana or Trello, to streamline workflows, allocate resources effectively, and ensure timely completion of tasks.

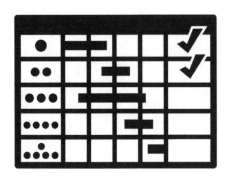

- **Communication Platforms**: Effective communication lies at the heart of successful leadership. Investing in communication platforms like Slack or Microsoft Teams fostered seamless collaboration among team members, enabling swift decision-making and fostering a culture of transparency and accountability.

Practical Tip: Implement a centralised project management system to keep track of tasks, deadlines, and progress. Encourage regular communication and feedback sessions to ensure alignment and cohesion within the team.

As an Entrepreneur:

- **Business Management Tools:**

Entrepreneurship demands a multifaceted approach to business management. I leveraged tools like QuickBooks or Xero for financial management, enabling me to track expenses, manage invoices, and gain insights into cash flow.

- **Productivity Apps:**

Maximising productivity is essential for entrepreneurs wearing multiple hats. I integrated productivity apps like Todoist or Evernote into my workflow to organise tasks, set priorities, and stay focused amidst competing demands.

- **Continuous Learning Resources:**

Entrepreneurship is a journey of perpetual growth and learning. I cultivated a habit of continuous learning by subscribing to platforms like LinkedIn Learning or Coursera, accessing a wealth of courses and resources to enhance my skills and knowledge base.

Practical Tip: Invest time in exploring and mastering the tools that best suit your business needs and personal preferences. Regularly review and update your toolkit to stay abreast of emerging trends and technologies.

By aligning your toolkit with the demands of management and entrepreneurship, you not only optimised efficiency but also created a fertile ground for creativity and innovation. Embracing the right tools has empowered me to navigate challenges with confidence, seize opportunities for growth, and chart a course towards success in the ever-evolving landscape of business.

Tools Decluttering Checklist

- ✅ Step 1: Conduct a Tool Audit
- ✅ Step 2: Categorise Your Tools
- ✅ Step 3: Simplify and Streamline
- ✅ Step 4: Master Your Chosen Tools
- ✅ Step 5: Regularly Review and Adapt

Tools Decluttering Checklist

Step 1: Conduct a Tool Audit

- List Your Tools: Start by listing all the tools you currently use across all devices and physical spaces. Include everything from digital apps to physical instruments relevant to your work.

- Evaluate Usefulness: For each tool, ask yourself: When was the last time I used this? Does it significantly contribute to my productivity or creativity? This evaluation helps identify which tools are essential and which are superfluous.

Tools Decluttering Checklist

Step 2: Categorise Your Tools

Group your tools into three categories to better understand their roles and importance in your workflow:

1. Digital Tools for Mobile Devices: These should include apps that you use on the go, helping you stay connected and productive anywhere.

2. Software and Tools for Your Laptop/Desktop: Focus on tools that are crucial for your main work processes, such as project management software or specialised applications for your field.

3. Physical Tools: Identify the tangible tools you rely on daily, whether it's a designer's sketchpad, a planner, or ergonomic office equipment.

Tools Decluttering Checklist

Step 3: Simplify and Streamline

- Reduce Redundancies: Eliminate duplicate tools serving similar purposes. Choose the one that best fits your workflow and needs.

- Prioritise Integration: Opt for tools that integrate well with each other, simplifying your process and reducing the need to switch contexts frequently.

Tools Decluttering Checklist

Step 4: Master Your Chosen Tools

- Dedicate Time to Learn: Invest time in tutorials, courses, or webinars to fully understand the capabilities of your selected tools.

- Explore Advanced Features: Many tools offer advanced features that users often overlook. Delve into these to maximise the tool's potential.

Tools Decluttering Checklist

Step 5: Regularly Review and Adapt

- Schedule Bi-Annual Reviews: Technology and needs evolve; regularly reassess your toolset to ensure it remains aligned with your goals.

- Stay Open to Change: Be willing to adopt new tools that offer significant improvements over your current set, but always through the lens of enhancing quality and efficiency.

Tools for High Achievers Across Sectors:

Disclaimer:

Just a quick heads up before we get into the nitty-gritty of these tools—I'm not in the business of endorsing any specific software brands here. My aim is simply to share insights based on my own experiences as someone who strives to excel. These tools have been integral to my daily workflow and I've found them incredibly effective. However, it's important to remember that everyone's needs are different, so while these might be great for me, your mileage may vary. Consider this a starting point to discover what tools align best with your personal or professional goals. Let's dive in!

Tools for High Achievers Across Sectors:

1. Notion or Trello for Project Management:
Both platforms offer a versatile environment for managing projects, tasks, and collaborations, with the flexibility to adapt to various workflows.

2. Grammarly for Writing Assistance:
A tool that transcends sectors, Grammarly helps ensure your written communication is clear, effective, and error-free, whether you're drafting a design proposal or a business plan.

3. Canva for Design Needs:
For professionals in any sector, Canva provides an easy-to-use platform for creating professional-grade visuals without needing extensive graphic design skills.

4. Slack or Microsoft Teams for Communication:
These communication platforms facilitate seamless collaboration and information sharing, allowing teams to stay connected regardless of their physical location. With features like instant messaging, file sharing, and video conferencing, they streamline communication and enhance productivity.

5. Google Workspace (formerly G Suite) for Productivity:

Google Workspace offers a suite of cloud-based productivity tools, including Gmail, Google Drive, Google Docs, Sheets, and Slides. These tools enable seamless collaboration in real-time, allowing high achievers to work efficiently on documents, spreadsheets, and presentations from anywhere, on any device.

6. LinkedIn for Networking and Professional Development:

As a hub for professionals across industries, LinkedIn provides valuable opportunities for networking, knowledge-sharing, and career advancement. High achievers can leverage LinkedIn to expand their professional network, showcase their expertise, and stay informed about industry trends and opportunities.

7. Evernote for Note-taking and Organization:

Evernote is a powerful note-taking app that allows users to capture ideas, organise thoughts, and collaborate on projects. With features like tags, notebooks, and search functionality, Evernote helps high achievers stay organised and productive, whether they're brainstorming ideas, conducting research, or managing tasks.

8. Zoom or Microsoft Teams for Virtual Meetings:

In an increasingly remote work environment, virtual meeting platforms like Zoom and Microsoft Teams have become indispensable tools for high achievers. These platforms enable teams to conduct virtual meetings, webinars, and presentations with ease, fostering collaboration and communication across geographically dispersed teams.

Navigating the AI Revolution

The emergence of AI tools has ushered in a new era in the professional realm, presenting boundless possibilities for elevating efficiency and igniting creativity. With each passing day, we witness the evolution of AI applications that push the boundaries of innovation and redefine what's possible in our respective fields.

Take, for instance, the remarkable capabilities of ChatGPT in content creation. This AI-powered tool has revolutionized the way we generate written content, offering a seamless blend of human-like fluency and machine efficiency. Whether crafting blog posts, marketing copy, or social media content, ChatGPT empowers users to articulate their ideas with precision and flair.

Similarly, the advent of DALL·E 2 and Midjourney have opened new avenues for visual expression. This groundbreaking AI model is capable of generating lifelike images from textual descriptions, sparking the imagination and fueling creativity in fields ranging from graphic design to digital art. With Midjourney, the boundaries between imagination and reality blur, enabling users to bring their wildest visions to life with unprecedented realism.

Moreover, the coming of generative AI has heralded a new era of innovation and creativity. These advanced AI models, such as OpenAI's GPT-4, possess the ability to generate text, images, and even music autonomously. With generative AI, the creative process is no longer confined to human minds alone; instead, it becomes a collaborative effort between human creativity and machine intelligence.

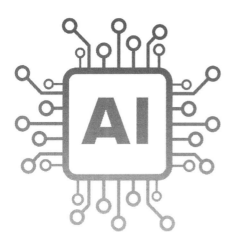
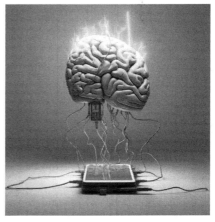

Meanwhile, specialised AI software like Notion AI has redefined productivity, offering intelligent assistance and automation to streamline workflows and optimise time management. By harnessing the power of AI, users can unlock new levels of efficiency and effectiveness in their daily tasks, from organising projects to managing schedules and prioritising tasks.

However, as we marvel at the transformative potential of AI, it's essential to recognise that the landscape is ever-evolving. The rapid pace of development means that what's cutting-edge today may be outdated tomorrow. Therefore, staying abreast of the latest tools and trends in AI technology is paramount for professionals seeking to harness its full potential.

In this age of constant innovation, a commitment to continuous learning and exploration is key. By remaining curious, adaptive, and open-minded, we can navigate the AI revolution with confidence, seizing opportunities for growth and innovation along the way.

Key Takeaways:

- The right tools, chosen with an emphasis on quality and relevance to your specific needs, can significantly enhance productivity and creativity across any sector.

- A streamlined toolset, focused on integration and mastery, reduces cognitive load, simplifies workflows, and allows for deeper focus and innovation.

- Regularly reviewing and adapting your choice of tools ensures that your arsenal remains efficient and aligned with your evolving professional landscape.

This practical guide aims to empower professionals across sectors to navigate the tool trap, emphasizing that a thoughtful, quality-focused approach to tool selection is essential for achieving high productivity and creative output in the modern workplace.

Chapter 5

"To master time, first master yourself; the true key to productivity lies in self-awareness and self-management."

Damian Tang

CHAPTER FIVE

Managing Self, Not Time

In my relentless pursuit of productivity, it becomes increasingly evident that the true challenge lies not in managing time itself, but rather in mastering the art of self-management. This pivotal chapter delves into the profound shift from time management to self-management, illuminating the crucial role of self-awareness, energy management, and insight into our internal motivations and obstacles.

At its core, self-management entails a deep understanding of our own psychological and emotional landscape, as well as the factors that influence our behaviour and decision-making. By cultivating self-awareness, we gain the ability to navigate challenges with clarity and purpose, steering our actions in alignment with our values and objectives.

Central to the concept of self-management is the recognition of decision fatigue—an all-too-common pitfall of attempting to micromanage every aspect of our lives. By categorising decisions into 'threat' and 'non-threat' categories, we can effectively conserve mental energy and focus our attention where it matters most. Moreover, empowering others to make decisions on non-critical matters not only lightens our cognitive load but also fosters a culture of trust, collaboration, and shared accountability.

Delegating Non-Threat Decisions:

Acknowledging the overwhelming cognitive load imposed by an incessant barrage of decisions, I made a conscious choice to decentralise decision-making authority. By empowering trusted individuals to autonomously address non-critical matters, I not only alleviated my own mental burden but also fostered a culture of collaboration and shared responsibility. This strategic delegation not only liberated me to focus on high-stakes endeavours but also empowered team members, cultivating a sense of ownership and investment in our collective success.

Pitfalls of Time Management vs. Self-Management:

While time management may seem like a logical approach to enhancing productivity, it often leads to a host of pitfalls and limitations. By fixating solely on the allocation of time, individuals may overlook the underlying factors that truly impact their effectiveness and well-being:

1. Rigidity and inflexibility:
Time management frameworks can sometimes breed rigidity, leaving little room for adaptability or spontaneity. In contrast, self-management allows for greater flexibility, enabling individuals to respond to changing circumstances with agility and resilience.

2. Burnout and exhaustion:
The relentless pursuit of productivity at the expense of self-care can result in burnout and exhaustion. Self-management prioritises holistic well-being, emphasising the importance of balancing work with rest, recreation, and personal fulfilment.

3. Lack of alignment with goals and values:
Time management strategies may focus solely on efficiency and output, without considering whether our actions are aligned with our overarching goals and values. Self-management encourages introspection and alignment, ensuring that our efforts are directed toward meaningful pursuits that resonate with our core beliefs and aspirations.

4. Ineffective prioritisation:
Time management techniques often prioritise tasks based solely on urgency or deadline, rather than considering their true importance or impact. In contrast, self-management involves discerning between 'busy work' and truly meaningful endeavours, allocating time and resources accordingly.

My Journey to Self-Management

Embarking on the path of self-management unveiled profound insights into the intricacies of decision-making, illuminating the need for a nuanced approach beyond mere time allocation. Here's how I navigated this transformative journey:

Checklist for Decision-Making:

1. Identify Priority Decisions: Determine which decisions are critical to your goals and objectives, distinguishing between urgent, high-impact choices and those of lesser consequence.

2. Assess Risks and Rewards: Evaluate the potential risks and rewards associated with each decision, considering short-term and long-term implications.

3. Gather Information: Gather relevant data and insights to inform your decision-making process, seeking input from trusted sources and experts when necessary.

4. Consider Alternatives: Explore alternative courses of action, weighing the pros and cons of each option to make an informed choice.

5. Set Criteria: Establish clear criteria or benchmarks to guide your decision-making, ensuring alignment with your values, priorities, and objectives.

6. Evaluate Impact: Anticipate the potential impact of your decision on yourself, your team, and your organization, considering both immediate and long-term consequences.

7. Take Action: Make a definitive choice based on your analysis and deliberation, committing to follow through with confidence and conviction.

8. Review and Learn: Reflect on the outcomes of your decisions, identifying lessons learned and areas for improvement to refine your decision-making process in the future.

Learning from Baumeister and Tierney

The insights gleaned from the pioneering work of Baumeister and Tierney on willpower as a finite resource shed light on the intricacies of self-control and decision-making. Central to their research is the notion that willpower functions much like a muscle—it can be strengthened with practice, but it also has its limits.

Baumeister and Tierney's seminal book, "Willpower: Rediscovering the Greatest Human Strength," elucidates the finite resource model of willpower, which posits that our capacity for self-control diminishes over time as we expend mental energy throughout the day. This depletion of willpower can manifest in various ways, from succumbing to temptations to experiencing difficulty in maintaining focus and concentration.

Implications for Self-Management over Time Management

The finite resource model indicates that simply managing your time efficiently isn't enough for high achievement. Since willpower depletes over time, it's crucial to prioritise tasks that require the most self-control or focus earlier in the day when your willpower reservoir is fuller. This shifts the emphasis from just managing time to managing energy and willpower effectively.

To illustrate the practical implications of this concept, let's explore ten scenarios in our daily lives where strategic decision-making and the effective allocation of mental energy are paramount:

1. Morning Routine: Deciding whether to hit the snooze button or wake up immediately sets the tone for the rest of the day. By exerting willpower to resist the temptation of extra sleep, we conserve mental energy for more consequential decisions later on.

2. Healthy Eating Choices: Choosing between a nutritious salad and a greasy fast-food meal requires self-control and willpower. By opting for the healthier option, we prioritise long-term health over short-term gratification.

3. Exercise Regimen: Motivating oneself to stick to a regular exercise routine often requires a significant amount of willpower. By establishing a consistent schedule and minimising decision fatigue, we make it easier to maintain our fitness goals.

4. Work Environment: Creating a conducive work environment free from distractions can help preserve mental energy and enhance productivity. By minimising clutter and implementing effective time management strategies, we optimise our focus and concentration.

5. Task Prioritisation: Determining which tasks to tackle first can be challenging, especially when faced with competing demands. By utilising prioritisation techniques such as the Eisenhower Matrix, we allocate our limited willpower to tasks that align with our goals and objectives.

6. Social Interactions: Navigating social situations requires diplomacy and self-control. By setting boundaries and managing expectations, we conserve mental energy for meaningful interactions and avoid unnecessary conflicts.

7. Digital Distractions: Resisting the allure of constant notifications and social media scrolling demands willpower. By implementing digital detox strategies and practicing mindfulness, we reclaim control over our attention and focus.

8. Financial Decisions: Exercising restraint in spending and budgeting requires discipline and self-control. By adhering to a budgeting plan and avoiding impulsive purchases, we safeguard our financial well-being.

9. Time Management: Juggling multiple tasks and deadlines can deplete mental energy rapidly. By employing time-blocking techniques and batching similar tasks together, we optimise productivity and minimise decision fatigue.

10. Evening Wind-Down: Deciding when to disconnect from work and unwind before bed is crucial for restful sleep. By establishing a relaxing bedtime routine and avoiding stimulating activities, we ensure that we recharge our mental energy for the challenges of the next day.

Incorporating the insights from Baumeister and Tierney's research into our daily lives empowers us to make more intentional choices, preserve our mental resources, and cultivate greater resilience in the face of challenges. By strategically managing our willpower, we can enhance our productivity, well-being, and overall quality of life.

In short, in order to better manage my willpower and energy, I adopted the following strategies:

Prioritise Tasks: Focus on tasks that have the most significant impact first when willpower is at its peak.
Minimise Decision Fatigue: Make fewer decisions by establishing routines or automating repetitive tasks.
Empower Others: Delegate 'non-threat' decisions to conserve energy for more critical tasks.
Be Easy on Yourself: Accept that not all decisions need your input, and let go of trivial matters.

Takeaway: Finding Your Rhythm

Understanding and applying a mindset that prioritises significant decisions while delegating or dismissing lesser ones is crucial for effective self-management. By focusing on 'threat' versus 'non-threat' decisions, we can better utilise our energy and willpower, achieving a more balanced and fulfilling life.

Daily Tools for Self-Management: A Step-by-Step Guide

Decision Matrix: Categorising Decisions

1. Create Your Matrix:
Draw a two-by-two grid on a piece of paper or digital app. Label the axes as 'Impact' (High/Low) and 'Urgency' (High/Low).

2. List Decisions:
Write down the decisions you need to make.

3. Categorise Each Decision:
Place each decision in the appropriate quadrant based on its impact on your goals (high or low) and its urgency (immediate or can wait).

4. Prioritise:
Focus first on decisions in the High Impact/High Urgency quadrant. Delegate or schedule decisions in the Low Impact quadrants when possible.

Delegation List: Streamlining Task Assignment

1. Identify Delegable Tasks:
Review your to-do list and highlight tasks that do not require your specific expertise.

2. Choose Delegates:
Think about your team or family members' strengths and interests. Match tasks to individuals accordingly.

3. Communicate Clearly:
When delegating, be clear about the task requirements, deadlines, and why you've chosen them for this task. Provide resources or support as needed.

4. Follow-up:
Set a reminder to check in on progress before the deadline. Offer assistance or clarification if needed, but avoid micromanaging.

Routines for Trivial Decisions: Simplifying Daily Choices

1. Identify Repetitive Decisions:
Make a list of daily or weekly decisions that consume your time but have little impact on your overall productivity (e.g., what to wear, what to eat for breakfast).

2. Develop Routines:
Create routines that eliminate these decisions. For example, plan your outfits for the week every Sunday or have the same breakfast on weekdays.

3. Automate Where Possible:
Use technology to automate decisions. For instance, set recurring online grocery orders for staples or use app reminders for regular tasks.

4. Evaluate and Adjust:
After a few weeks, review these routines. Adjust them if they're not reducing decision fatigue or if your circumstances change.

Implementing Your Self-Management Tools

- Start Small: Begin with one tool and gradually incorporate others into your routine.
- Regular Reviews: At the end of each week, evaluate which tools were most effective and why. Use this insight to refine your approach.
- Be Flexible: Your needs and tasks will evolve. Adapt your use of these tools as necessary to remain effective and efficient.

Key Takeaways for Enhanced Self-Management

- Effective self-management relies on strategic decision-making and task delegation. Utilising tools like a decision matrix and a delegation list can significantly reduce cognitive overload and improve productivity.
- Establishing routines for trivial decisions frees up mental energy for more critical tasks, enhancing focus and efficiency.
- Regular review and adaptation of your self-management tools are crucial to ensure they meet your evolving needs and continue to facilitate a balanced, productive lifestyle.
- True productivity stems from managing oneself, distinguishing between critical and non-critical decisions.
- Empowering others to handle non-essential decisions fosters collaboration and reduces decision fatigue.
- Learning to let go of minor concerns is essential for focusing willpower on what truly matters.

Chapter 6

"Comfort breeds complacency, and procrastination is its offspring; embrace discomfort, and watch productivity flourish."

Damian Tang

CHAPTER SIX

Comfort, Procrastination, and Their Discontents

On our path of growth, we often encounter sneaky obstacles like seeking comfort and putting things off. These may seem harmless at first, but they can trap us in a rut, affecting how we feel, how we connect with others, and how we advance in our careers. Drawing from my own journey and delving into the science behind it all, I want to shed light on how these habits can silently chip away at us. Plus, I'll share some tips on how to break free from their grip.

The Lure of Comfort and Procrastination

The seductive nature of comfort often lulls us into complacency, hindering growth, while procrastination misleads us with the illusion of limitless time, creating a cycle of inaction. This cycle not only delays progress but also erodes self-esteem and strains our relationships, leaving us battling regret and a diminished sense of self-worth.

1. The Comfort Trap: Imagine you have a goal to start a daily exercise routine. However, each morning, the allure of staying cozy in bed persuades you to hit the snooze button rather than hitting the gym. While it feels nice in the moment, over time, this comfort keeps you from reaching your fitness goals and may even lead to feelings of dissatisfaction with your health and body.

2. Procrastination's Illusion: You have a work project with a deadline two weeks away. Instead of starting right away, you tell yourself you have plenty of time and spend the first few days browsing the internet or watching TV. As the deadline approaches, you find yourself scrambling to complete the project, feeling stressed and overwhelmed. Procrastination tricked you into thinking you had limitless time, but now you're facing the consequences of your inaction.

3. Strained Relationships: You've been meaning to catch up with a friend for weeks, but every time you think about reaching out, you convince yourself that you'll do it later. Meanwhile, your friend feels neglected and begins to wonder if you even care about the friendship. Your procrastination in reaching out strains the relationship, leading to misunderstandings and hurt feelings on both sides.

4. Battle with Self-Esteem: You've been wanting to learn a new skill or hobby for a while now, but every time you consider starting, doubts creep in. You tell yourself you're not good enough or that you'll never succeed, so why bother trying? This negative self-talk fueled by procrastination and fear of stepping out of your comfort zone eats away at your self-esteem, making it even harder to take action and pursue your passions.

In these everyday examples, we can see how the lure of comfort and the trap of procrastination can subtly impact our lives, delaying progress, straining relationships, and eroding our sense of self-worth.

Understanding the Roots

Neurological Factors:
Think of your brain like a complex machine with different parts responsible for different tasks. When it comes to making decisions, sometimes the part of your brain in charge of planning (the prefrontal cortex) gets overruled by another part (the limbic system) that's all about emotions and rewards. So, when faced with a choice between doing something uncomfortable now or enjoying a quick pleasure, like scrolling through social media, your brain often goes for the immediate gratification, even if it's not the best choice in the long run.

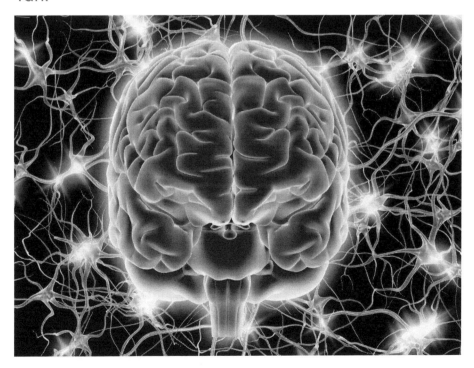

Psychological Factors:
Picture this: you have this dream you want to pursue, but every time you think about taking a step forward, there's this nagging feeling of fear. It's like a little voice in your head saying, "What if you fail?" or "What if you succeed, and things change?" These fears can hold you back, making you stick to what's familiar and comfortable, even if it's not what you really want. It's like your mind builds these walls, keeping you from embracing new opportunities and experiences.

So, when you find yourself putting things off or sticking to your comfort zone, it's not just about being lazy or lacking motivation. There's this whole intricate dance going on inside your brain, where emotions and fears often take the lead, making it hard to break free and take action. But understanding these roots can be the first step towards overcoming them and living a more fulfilling life.

The Toll of Inaction

The mental and relational toll of dwelling in comfort zones and succumbing to procrastination is profound. Mentally, it fosters guilt and anxiety, while relationally, it leads to unfulfilled obligations and isolation, eroding trust and mutual respect in our relationships.

Mental Toll:
Imagine you keep putting off something important, like studying for an exam or tackling a big project at work. As time passes, you start feeling this weight on your shoulders, a mix of guilt and anxiety. You know you should be doing something, but you keep avoiding it, and

that nagging feeling just won't go away. It's like there's this cloud hanging over your head, making it hard to focus and enjoy anything else because you're constantly worrying about what you're not doing.

Relational Toll:
Now, think about how this habit of procrastination and sticking to your comfort zone affects your relationships. Maybe you keep canceling plans with friends or forgetting to follow through on promises you made to loved ones. Each time you do this, it chips away at the trust and mutual respect in those relationships. Your friends and family start to feel let down and may even start pulling away because they can't rely on you anymore. Soon enough, you find yourself feeling isolated, like you're drifting further and further away from the people who matter most to you.

So, it's not just about missing deadlines or skipping out on social events. Staying stuck in our comfort zones and procrastinating can have a deep impact on our mental well-being and the quality of our relationships, leaving us feeling burdened with guilt and anxiety while pushing away the people we care about.

Strategies for Overcoming Comfort and Procrastination

- Acknowledge the Fear: Identify and confront the underlying fears that drive procrastination.
- Break Tasks into Smaller Steps: Tackle overwhelm by dividing larger tasks into manageable actions.
- Set Clear Deadlines: Create urgency with self-imposed deadlines for each task.
- Embrace Discomfort: Growth lies beyond comfort zones. Challenge yourself with new tasks and experiences.
- Develop Accountability Systems: Share your goals with trusted individuals who can offer support and hold you accountable.
- Practice Mindfulness: Enhance self-awareness and manage anxiety through mindfulness, improving decision-making.
- Reward Progress: Celebrate milestones to reinforce positive behavior and progress.

Implementing Change

Transitioning from the familiar territory of comfort and procrastination to a more proactive and growth-oriented mindset is not an overnight shift; it's a journey of gradual transformation. Embracing change requires patience, resilience, and a steadfast commitment to stepping beyond the boundaries of comfort, even when faced with setbacks.

Each small step taken towards overcoming inertia and embracing new challenges is a triumph against stagnation. It's about consistently nudging yourself beyond the confines of what feels safe and familiar, even when the allure of comfort beckons. It's about acknowledging that change is often messy and nonlinear, but every effort invested in pushing past comfort zones is a testament to your resilience and determination.

So, as you embark on this journey of self-discovery and growth, remember to be gentle with yourself. Celebrate the progress you make, no matter how small, and recognise that every moment of discomfort is an opportunity for growth. With patience, persistence, and a willingness to embrace the unknown, you'll find yourself gradually breaking free from the grip of comfort and procrastination, paving the way for a more fulfilling and purpose-driven life.

Simple steps to encourage yourself as you implement change:

1. Set Small, Achievable Goals: Break down your goals into smaller, manageable steps. Focus on taking one step at a time, celebrating each accomplishment along the way.

2. Practice Self-Compassion: Be kind to yourself throughout this process. Understand that setbacks are a natural part of growth, and treat yourself with patience and understanding.

3. Stay Consistent: Consistency is key to making lasting changes. Commit to taking small actions consistently, even when faced with challenges or setbacks.

4. Celebrate Progress: Take time to acknowledge and celebrate the progress you make, no matter how small. Celebrating milestones reinforces positive behaviour and keeps you motivated.

5. Embrace Discomfort: Understand that discomfort is a natural part of growth. Instead of avoiding it, lean into it and see it as an opportunity for learning and development.

6. Stay Mindful: Practice mindfulness to stay present and grounded during moments of discomfort or uncertainty. Mindfulness can help you manage stress and anxiety, making it easier to navigate change.

7. Seek Support: Surround yourself with a supportive network of friends, family, or mentors who can encourage and uplift you on your journey. Don't be afraid to reach out for help when needed.

8. Stay Patient and Persistent: Remember that change takes time, and progress may not always be linear. Stay patient and persistent, and trust in your ability to overcome challenges and reach your goals.

Remember, every small step you take towards growth is a victory worth celebrating.

Key Takeaways

Comfort and Procrastination's Impact:

It's easy to fall into the trap of seeking comfort and procrastinating on important tasks. But as enticing as they may seem in the moment, these habits can take a toll on our mental well-being and our relationships. They create this invisible barrier that keeps us from reaching our full potential and enjoying meaningful connections with others. It's like we're stuck in this cycle of inertia, where each day feels like a struggle to break free from the gravitational pull of familiarity and avoidance.

Empowerment through Understanding:

However, knowledge is power, and by delving into the neurological and psychological roots of comfort and procrastination, we gain valuable insights that can empower us to take back control of our lives. It's like shining a light into the dark corners of our minds, uncovering the hidden mechanisms that drive our behavior. Armed with this understanding, we can start to devise effective counter-strategies to combat these self-limiting tendencies.

Embracing Action and Accountability:

But understanding alone isn't enough; we must also take action. Breaking down our goals into smaller, manageable steps makes them feel less daunting and more achievable. And by fostering accountability —whether through sharing our goals with trusted friends or utilizing accountability apps—we create a support system that keeps us accountable and motivated.

Stepping into Discomfort and Mindfulness:

Growth doesn't happen in the comfort zone; it happens when we push ourselves beyond our limits and embrace discomfort. It's about leaning into the unknown, knowing that it's where true growth lies. And mindfulness serves as our compass on this journey, helping us stay grounded in the present moment, manage stress and anxiety, and make more intentional choices.

In essence, overcoming comfort and procrastination isn't just about changing our habits; it's about cultivating a mindset of growth and resilience. It's about embracing the challenges that come with stepping outside our comfort zones and trusting in our ability to navigate them. And with each small step we take towards this goal, we inch closer to becoming the best versions of ourselves.

Case Study: Transforming Alex, the Landscape Architect

Background: Alex, a landscape architect with a keen eye for design and a deep appreciation for nature, found himself in a professional rut. Despite his talent and creativity, Alex was not advancing in his career. He attributed this stagnation to his habitual procrastination and preference for staying within his comfort zone, which had led to missed project opportunities and a general sense of unfulfilment.

Initial Assessment: During our initial meetings, it became apparent that Alex's procrastination stemmed from deeper issues rather than mere disorganisation or laziness. A significant factor was his fear of failure, compounded by an unwillingness to step out of his comfort zone, which hindered his professional growth and innovation in design.

Over the years, I have had the privilege of mentoring numerous professionals in the fields of architecture and landscape architecture. These creative and visionary individuals often come to me with a common set of challenges—navigating the complex path of career growth, overcoming creative blocks, and, more frequently than one might expect, battling the twin foes of comfort and procrastination. My role as a mentor has evolved into not just guiding them through the technicalities of their profession but also coaching them on how to harness their full potential by breaking through psychological barriers that hinder their progress.

Among these mentees, Alex's story stands out as emblematic of a talented individual whose journey was impeded by his tendency to seek comfort and delay tasks. Alex, a landscape architect from Malaysia with a natural flair for innovative design and a deep respect for the environment, found himself in a professional standstill, unable to advance his career or fully express his creative abilities. This stagnation, as we discovered, was not due to a lack of skill or opportunity but stemmed from a deeper struggle with procrastination and a reluctance to step out of his comfort zone.

My coaching approach with Alex, as with many of my mentees in architecture and landscape architecture, focused on identifying the underlying causes of his procrastination and comfort-seeking behaviours. We worked together to develop strategies that addressed these issues head-on, enabling him to rediscover his passion for design, take on challenging projects with confidence, and ultimately, achieve a level of professional satisfaction and growth he had previously thought unattainable.

Alex's transformation is a testament to the power of personalised mentorship and the importance of addressing not just the technical skills but also the mental and emotional barriers that professionals in creative fields often face. It highlights the critical role of mentorship in unlocking the potential within each individual, guiding them through their struggles with comfort and procrastination, and steering them towards a more fulfilling career path.

Strategy Implementation:

1. **Addressing the Root Causes:** We began by identifying and discussing Alex's fears and how they were impacting his work. Alex realised that his procrastination was a protective mechanism against the possibility of his designs being critiqued or rejected.

2. **Task Segmentation for Complex Projects:** Alex often felt overwhelmed by large-scale design projects, leading him to delay starting them. Together, we broke these projects into smaller, actionable steps, assigning realistic deadlines to each segment to foster a sense of progress and achievement.

3. **Challenging the Comfort Zone:** I encouraged Alex to undertake at least one project or task each week that pushed him beyond his usual scope of work. This could range from experimenting with a new design software to incorporating unconventional materials into his designs.

4. **Establishing Accountability:** We set up weekly check-ins where Alex would share his progress, challenges, and insights. These sessions served as a motivational tool and helped Alex stay committed to his goals.

5. **Incorporating Mindfulness:** To help Alex deal with the anxiety linked to his fear of failure, we introduced mindfulness techniques. Practicing mindfulness helped him to focus better, reduce stress, and approach his design work with a clearer mind.

Outcome: Over the course of several months, Alex made significant strides. He successfully completed an innovative public park project that had been in limbo, received commendation for his unique approach to sustainable design, and led a community workshop on eco-friendly landscaping practices. His confidence grew not only in his professional abilities but also in his personal life, where he began exploring new hobbies related to environmental conservation. His design skills were so exceptional that he was headhunted by an American landscape architecture company and migrated there.

Reflection: Alex's transformation underscored the importance of confronting personal fears, breaking tasks into manageable steps, and stepping out of comfort zones as pathways to growth. The strategies we implemented demonstrated the effectiveness of personalised coaching in overcoming deep-seated habits of procrastination and comfort-seeking.

Key Takeaways for Alex:

- **Embracing New Challenges:** Venturing beyond familiar territories unlocked Alex's creative potential and led to groundbreaking work.

- **Structured Approach to Complex Projects:** Segmenting tasks made daunting projects more approachable and less overwhelming.

- **The Power of Accountability:** Regular progress reviews kept Alex motivated and focused on his objectives.

- **Stress Management Through Mindfulness:** Adopting mindfulness practices enabled Alex to tackle anxiety and maintain a sharper focus on his designs.

Alex's journey from stagnation to growth in the field of landscape architecture serves as an inspiring example of how targeted strategies and support can help individuals break through barriers of comfort and procrastination to reach new heights in their careers.

Key Takeaways from this case study:

- **Embracing New Challenges:** Just like Alex, stepping out of your comfort zone can unlock hidden talents and lead to remarkable achievements. Don't be afraid to try something new and push yourself beyond what feels safe and familiar.

- **Structured Approach to Complex Projects:** Breaking down daunting tasks into smaller, more manageable steps can make even the most overwhelming projects feel achievable. By taking a structured approach, you can tackle challenges with confidence and clarity.

- **The Power of Accountability:** Accountability can be a powerful motivator on your journey towards personal and professional growth. Whether it's sharing your goals with a friend, joining a support group, or using accountability tools, having someone to hold you accountable can keep you on track and focused on your objectives.

- **Stress Management Through Mindfulness:** Incorporating mindfulness practices into your daily routine can help you manage stress, anxiety, and distractions more effectively. By staying present and centered, you can maintain a sharper focus on your goals and overcome obstacles with greater ease.

Alex's transformation from a place of stagnation to one of growth and success serves as a testament to the potential within each of us to break free from the shackles of comfort and procrastination. With determination, perseverance, and the right strategies in place, anyone can follow in Alex's footsteps and achieve their own version of success.

Chapter 7

"In the battle between old and new productivity paradigms, innovation is the weapon of the future high achiever."

Damian Tang

CHAPTER SEVEN

Old Versus New Productivity Paradigms

As I navigate the ever-changing terrain of productivity, I find myself reflecting on a journey marked by profound transformation. This chapter serves as a personal exploration of my evolution from relying on traditional methods of productivity to embracing the innovative, neuroscience-informed strategies that characterise the digital age. It's not just a recounting of techniques; it's a narrative of adaptation, growth, and the quest for a more efficient path towards realising my goals in the whirlwind of today's fast-paced world.

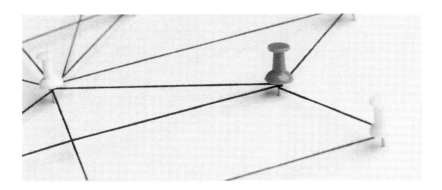

From the outset, I was steeped in the wisdom of time-tested productivity techniques. I adhered faithfully to the principles laid out in classic self-help books, diligently crafting to-do lists and prioritising tasks based on urgency and importance. Yet, as the demands of modern life intensified and technology reshaped the way we work and interact, I found myself grappling with a sense of overwhelm and inefficiency. The old methods, once reliable guides, began to feel inadequate in the face of relentless digital distractions and information overload.

It was amidst this backdrop of uncertainty and frustration that I embarked on a journey of discovery, seeking out new approaches rooted in the latest findings from neuroscience and psychology. I devoured articles, attended workshops, and experimented with a myriad of productivity tools and techniques, eager to unlock the secrets of peak performance in the digital age.

What emerged from this period of exploration was a profound shift in mindset and methodology. I learned to harness the power of neuroplasticity, rewiring my brain to better cope with the demands of modern life. I embraced the principles of cognitive flexibility, learning to adapt and pivot in the face of uncertainty. And I discovered the transformative potential of mindfulness, finding solace in moments of quiet amidst the chaos of the digital world.

But perhaps most importantly, I learned to embrace experimentation and iteration as essential components of the productivity journey. No longer bound by rigid systems or dogmatic approaches, I embraced a mindset of continuous improvement, constantly refining and optimising my strategies based on feedback and experience.

As I reflect on this evolution, I am struck by the profound impact it has had on both my personal and professional life. I am more focused, more resilient, and more equipped to navigate the challenges of the modern world. And while the journey is far from over, I am filled with a sense of optimism and excitement for the possibilities that lie ahead. For in the ever-evolving landscape of productivity, the only constant is change—and with it, the opportunity for growth and transformation.

The Beginning: Traditional Productivity

My journey into the realm of productivity commenced with the tried-and-tested methods that have long been ingrained in our collective consciousness. I diligently adhered to structured schedules, meticulously crafted to-do lists, and upheld the unwavering ethos of the 9-to-5 workday. These principles, reminiscent of a bygone era steeped in the rigidity of the industrial age, championed discipline and a standardised approach to task management. Armed with these time-honoured techniques, I embarked on my quest for efficiency and effectiveness in the realm of work.

However, as the winds of change swept through the landscape of modernity, ushering in the era of the digital revolution, cracks began to appear in the foundation of these traditional productivity methods. The relentless march of technological advancement brought with it a tidal wave of complexities and challenges, rendering the once stalwart strategies increasingly inadequate in their ability to cope with the evolving demands of contemporary work environments.

The digital age brought about a seismic shift in the way we work, communicate, and interact with information. The boundaries between work and leisure blurred as emails flooded our inboxes at all hours, and the allure of endless scrolling on social media beckoned from the glowing screens of our devices. In the face of this onslaught of distractions and disruptions, the traditional methods of productivity faltered, struggling to adapt to the fast-paced, interconnected world in which we now found ourselves.

What once served as guiding beacons of efficiency now seemed like relics of a bygone era, ill-equipped to navigate the complexities of the digital age. The rigid structures of structured schedules and exhaustive to-do lists buckled under the weight of information overload, leaving us feeling overwhelmed and ill-prepared to tackle the ever-expanding array of tasks and responsibilities that lay before us.

As I grappled with the limitations of these traditional productivity methods, I realised that the time had come for a new approach. It was time to embrace the transformative potential of the digital revolution and chart a new course towards productivity—one that would not only meet the challenges of the modern world but thrive amidst its complexities. And thus began the next chapter in my journey: the quest for innovative, neuroscience-informed strategies that would redefine the way I approached work and productivity in the digital age.

hours, and the allure of endless scrolling on social media beckoned from the glowing screens of our devices. In the face of this onslaught of distractions and disruptions, the traditional methods of productivity faltered, struggling to adapt to the fast-paced, interconnected world in which we now found ourselves.

What once served as guiding beacons of efficiency now seemed like relics of a bygone era, ill-equipped to navigate the complexities of the digital age. The rigid structures of structured schedules and exhaustive to-do lists buckled under the weight of information overload, leaving us feeling overwhelmed and ill-prepared to tackle the ever-expanding array of tasks and responsibilities that lay before us.

As I grappled with the limitations of these traditional productivity methods, I realised that the time had come for a new approach. It was time to embrace the transformative potential of the digital revolution and chart a new course towards productivity—one that would not only meet the challenges of the modern world but thrive amidst its complexities. And thus began the next chapter in my journey: the quest for innovative, neuroscience-informed strategies that would redefine the way I approached work and productivity in the digital age.

A Shift in Perspective: Discovering a New Approach

The turning point in my journey towards a more effective productivity philosophy arrived unexpectedly, nestled within the pages of Barbara Oakley's transformative book, "A Mind For Numbers". As I immersed myself in Oakley's exploration of cognitive science and learning strategies, a profound shift in perspective began to unfold. It was as if a veil had been lifted, revealing a new world of possibilities for enhancing productivity and problem-solving.

Oakley's insights resonated with me on a deeply personal level, transcending the boundaries of academic disciplines. Her elucidation of how different modes of thinking—focused and diffused—can synergise to optimise learning and creativity struck a chord within my psyche. This wasn't merely a discourse on mathematical principles or scientific theories; it was a profound revelation of universal truths that could revolutionise the way we approach productivity and personal growth.

Drawing from my own experiences, I found myself nodding in recognition as Oakley delved into the intricate workings of the human brain. I recalled moments of intense concentration, where I delved deep into a task, and contrasted them with periods of seemingly aimless wandering, where my thoughts meandered freely. What Oakley illuminated was the symbiotic relationship between these two modes of thinking—a dynamic interplay that could be harnessed to unlock new realms of productivity and creativity.

As I delved deeper into Oakley's teachings, I became increasingly fascinated by the neuroscience underpinning her insights. She deftly navigated the complex terrain of the brain, elucidating how neural networks are primed for both focused attention and diffuse reflection. This understanding, rooted in rigorous scientific research, served as a beacon of clarity amidst the sea of productivity advice inundating the digital landscape.

The revelation that productivity wasn't merely a matter of discipline and rigour, but also of giving our brains the space to make unexpected connections, was nothing short of revolutionary. It was a paradigm shift that transformed my approach to work and problem-solving, infusing it with a newfound sense of dynamism and creativity. Armed with Oakley's neuroscience-informed strategies, I embarked on a journey of self-discovery and innovation, eager to unlock the boundless potential of the human mind.

Adapting to the Digital Age

Embracing this new paradigm meant rethinking my daily routine. Instead of a rigid schedule, I began experimenting with intervals of concentrated work followed by deliberate breaks. This strategy wasn't just about resting; it was strategically leveraging relaxation to activate my brain's diffused mode, sparking creativity and innovation.

This approach aligns perfectly with the demands of the digital era, where adaptability and rapid learning are key. Modern productivity isn't a rigid framework but a fluid, dynamic process that integrates digital tools with a deep understanding of our cognitive rhythms.

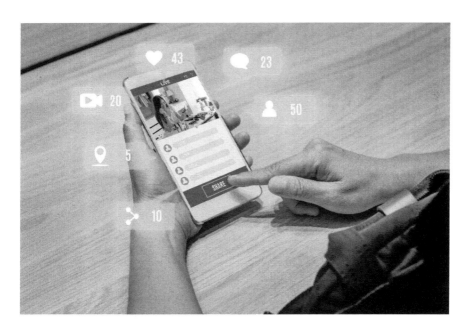

Finding Your Productivity Rhythm: A Step-by-Step Guide

To truly harness the power of modern productivity paradigms, it's crucial to find your unique rhythm—a blend of focused and diffused thinking tailored to your personal and professional life. Here's a straightforward, step-by-step guide to help you discover and implement this balanced approach.

Step 1: Understand Your Peaks and Troughs

Step 2: Embrace the Power of Breaks

Step 3: Leverage Technology Wisely

Step 4: Cultivate a Growth Mindset

Step 5: Create a Supportive Environment

Step 6: Prioritize Rest and Rejuvenation

Refer to the diagram on the next page for details.

Find Your Productivity Rhythm:
A Step-by-Step Guide

Know Your Productivity Rhythm in 7 Days

STEP 1: UNDERSTAND YOUR PEAKS AND TROUGHS

Track Your Energy: For one week, note the times of day when you feel most and least energised. Look for patterns to identify your peak productivity periods.

ALIGN TASKS WITH ENERGY LEVELS: SCHEDULE DEMANDING TASKS DURING YOUR HIGH-ENERGY PEAKS AND SAVE LOW-EFFORT ACTIVITIES FOR YOUR ENERGY TROUGHS.

NATURE BREAKS: INCORPORATE SHORT WALKS OR MOMENTS OUTSIDE INTO YOUR BREAK TIMES. NATURE CAN SIGNIFICANTLY BOOST YOUR DIFFUSED THINKING MODE, ENHANCING CREATIVITY.

STEP 2: EMBRACE THE POWER OF BREAKS

Pomodoro Technique: Try working in 25-minute intervals (Pomodoros), followed by a 5-minute break. After four Pomodoros, take a longer break of 15-30 minutes. This method helps maintain focus while ensuring regular rest.

STEP 3: LEVERAGE TECHNOLOGY WISELY

Digital Tools: Use apps and tools designed to enhance productivity. For example, note-taking apps can capture sudden insights during diffused thinking periods.

LIMIT DISTRACTIONS: UTILIZE WEBSITE BLOCKERS OR NOTIFICATION SETTINGS TO MINIMIZE DISTRACTIONS DURING FOCUSED WORK SESSIONS.

REFLECT AND ADAPT: AT THE END OF EACH WEEK, REFLECT ON WHAT WORKED WELL AND WHAT DIDN'T. ADJUST YOUR STRATEGIES ACCORDINGLY.

STEP 4: CULTIVATE A GROWTH MINDSET

Learning Goals: Set aside time each week to learn something new, related or unrelated to your work. This practice encourages neural plasticity and keeps you adaptable.

STEP 5: CREATE A SUPPORTIVE ENVIRONMENT

Physical Space: Organize your workspace to minimize clutter and maximize comfort, which can help reduce stress and improve focus.

SOCIAL SUPPORT: SHARE YOUR PRODUCTIVITY GOALS WITH FRIENDS, FAMILY, OR COLLEAGUES. THEY CAN OFFER ACCOUNTABILITY, SUPPORT, AND EVEN NEW STRATEGIES.

MINDFULNESS AND RELAXATION: PRACTICE MINDFULNESS, MEDITATION, OR OTHER RELAXATION TECHNIQUES DAILY. THESE PRACTICES HELP MANAGE STRESS AND PROMOTE MENTAL CLARITY.

STEP 6: PRIORITIZE REST AND REJUVENATION

Quality Sleep: Ensure you get enough restful sleep each night. Sleep is crucial for consolidating memories and rejuvenating your mind for another day of productive work.

WWW.URDXSTUDIO.COM/CIRCULAR-MIND/

Once you've uncovered your unique productivity rhythm, it's time to dive headfirst into action and put your insights into practice. This is where the magic happens—the moment when theory transforms into tangible results. It's about seizing the opportunity for self-optimisation and harnessing the power of your newfound knowledge to propel yourself towards greater efficiency and effectiveness.

Embrace the Self-Optimisation Action:

1. Plan and Think
2. Note it Down
3. Set 3 Tasks
4. Supporting Star
5. Visualise Goals
6. Think Again
7. Rest or Sleep
8. Reward Yourself

Refer to the diagram on the next page for details.

The moment you kickstart these actions, do them consistently for 7 days, and you will see the difference in your accelerated productivity.

SELF
OPTIMISATION

SEE THE DIFFERENCE IN 7 DAYS WHEN YOU MAKE THIS A DAILY HABIT

1. PLAN & THINK
Find the best time in the morning to plan and think for the day. It might be before or after breakfast. Or even while you eat or when you are jogging.

2. NOTE IT DOWN
DO not think that you can remember everything. Learn to note your thoughts in your notes app or physical notebook.

3. SET 3 TASKS
You may have many tasks to complete. But set 3 tasks to complete. Start with the easiest. Get one thing out of the way first. Add on later.

4. SUPPORTING STAR
What or who can support or boosts your morale? Music? 5min chat with your partner or colleague? Coffee? Sometimes simple things could do the magic.

5. VISUALISE GOALS
Previously you have set some tasks. Visualise what the completed tasks would be like. Would they make you less stress? Would they make your day? Have it in control.

6. THINK AGAIN
Morning thinking is not enough. Mid-day or end of day thinking may be another optimal time to rethink ideas and strategies. Find the best time that works for you.

7. REST OR SLEEP
Rest or sleep are not confine to the end of day. If power nap is needed, go for it. Go for a stroll or just pause and look out the window for greenery.

8. REWARD YOURSELF
You heard right. Reward yourself at the end of each day. It can be simple things that you like and can do without using much time. Keep your spirit high.

WWW.URDXSTUDIO.COM/CIRCULAR-MIND/

Key Takeaways: Embracing Modern Productivity

The journey from traditional productivity methods to a modern, neuroscience-backed approach underscores a crucial lesson: the way we work and learn must evolve alongside the world around us. By embracing the insights from neuroscience and integrating them with digital advancements, we craft a more adaptable and effective strategy for navigating the complexities of today's world.

- Flexibility Over Rigidity: Embrace a flexible approach to productivity that accommodates the natural ebb and flow of focused and diffused thinking.
- Harmony with Technology: Utilize digital tools not just for efficiency but as partners in optimizing our cognitive processes.
- Continuous Learning: Stay open to new insights from neuroscience and other fields to refine our strategies for success.

In essence, the evolution from old to new productivity paradigms is not just about adopting new tools or techniques; it's about a fundamental shift in how we understand and harness our cognitive capabilities.

Chapter 8

"To reach peak performance, become the master of your thoughts, emotions, and actions; for in mastering yourself, you unlock limitless potential."

Damian Tang

CHAPTER EIGHT

Mastery of Self for Peak Performance

In the quest for peak performance, the journey begins not with external achievements, but with an inward voyage towards self-awareness and mastery. Understanding our personal triggers, fears, and motivations is the key to unlocking our full potential. This chapter explores the profound impact of self-discovery on achieving high performance in all areas of life, underscored by personal anecdotes and grounded in the pioneering work of Daniel Goleman on emotional intelligence.

My Story: A Journey of Self-Discovery

My path to self-mastery has been deeply personal, marked by a constant balancing act between professional ambitions and the everyday dynamics of family life. Like any family, mine has its share of ups and downs, from the daily challenges of managing household chores, finances, and parenting to my young daughter at the same time navigating the emotional landscapes of marriage and personal relationships. These experiences, though seemingly mundane, are rife with moments that test our patience, resilience, and emotional intelligence.

In the midst of juggling work responsibilities and personal life, I've encountered numerous instances of frustration and dissatisfaction, leading to procrastination, low morale, and a noticeable dip in performance. It's in these moments that the importance of self-awareness becomes most evident. Recognising how our personal life affects our professional performance is crucial. The key lies in understanding that our reactions to daily stressors—whether it's my daughter ignoring requests or the strain of managing finances—can significantly impact our overall productivity and well-being.

As I stand on the threshold of this new chapter, I am drawn inward, to the depths of my own being. It is here, in the quiet recesses of self-discovery, that the journey towards peak performance truly begins. In the pages that follow, I invite you to join me on a deeply personal exploration—a voyage of introspection and transformation that has reshaped my understanding of success and fulfilment.

In this chapter, I peel back the layers of my soul, revealing not only my triumphs but also the darkest moments of my life. It is here, in the raw vulnerability of my struggles, that the

true power of self-mastery is revealed. For it is in confronting our deepest fears and overcoming our greatest challenges that we find the strength to rise above adversity and achieve our fullest potential.

I open my heart to you, sharing the tumultuous journey through the darkest valleys of my life. It was a time when despair and hopelessness gripped me tightly, threatening to drown me in their suffocating embrace.

The weight of the world pressed down on my shoulders with relentless force. The looming specter of cancer cast a shadow over our family as my mother battled the illness, each chemotherapy session draining us emotionally and financially. And as if that weren't enough, the COVID-19 pandemic unleashed a storm of financial turmoil, sending ripples of uncertainty through our lives.

The rising interest rates on our home loans, exacerbated by sweeping stimulus measures from US federal policy, threatened to pull us under, drowning us in a sea of debt. Meanwhile, the demands of renovating our new home and finalising payments for another property added fuel to the flames of our mounting stress.

But it wasn't just the financial strain that weighed heavily on my shoulders. The relentless demands of my role as president, coupled with the pressures of office politics, left me feeling stretched thin and utterly exhausted. And amidst it all, my wife battled her own demons, grappling with suspected depression under the crushing weight of family expectations.

Our home became a battleground, the air thick with tension and unspoken grievances. With each passing day, the divide between us grew wider, communication breaking down as resentment festered beneath the surface. Our once-loving partnership strained under the weight of unspoken burdens, leaving us adrift in a sea of loneliness and misunderstanding. The weight of stress and depressive symptoms bore down on me like a suffocating blanket, threatening to extinguish the light within me. It was only later, after seeking help from a psychiatrist, that I received a diagnosis: Adjustment Disorder with depressed mood (DSM-5 309.0).

As my personal challenges seeped into my professional realm, it felt like I was caught in a whirlpool, struggling to stay afloat. My once sharp focus dulled, and my productivity took a nosedive, leaving me feeling lost and overwhelmed. Procrastination became my constant companion, with every task feeling insurmountable in the face of mounting stress.

In the quiet hours of the night, when the world was hushed and my thoughts were my only company, I found myself seeking solace in unhealthy coping mechanisms. The clink of ice against glass and the numbing burn of alcohol offered a fleeting escape from the weight of my worries. Social media became my refuge, a digital oasis where I could lose myself in mindless scrolling, temporarily forgetting the turmoil of my reality.

Despite knowing the strain my financial situation was under, I found myself succumbing to impulsive online shopping sprees, rationalising each unnecessary purchase with the false promise that it "didn't cost much." It was as if I was trying to fill a void within myself with material possessions, hoping that the temporary thrill of acquiring something new would drown out the persistent whispers of self-doubt and anxiety.

But with each click of the "buy now" button, the grip of my bad habits tightened, pulling me further into a downward spiral of self-destructive behaviour. It was a cycle that seemed impossible to break, a tangled web of escapism and avoidance that only served to exacerbate my struggles.

In those moments of weakness, I realised that I was not only battling external challenges but also fighting against the demons within myself. It was a wake-up call—a stark reminder that true healing and growth could only begin once I confronted my innermost fears and insecurities head-on.

My inner voice began to whisper words of doubt and defeat, tricking me into believing that the world was unfair and that no one was supporting me. I convinced myself that I had the right to dwell deeper in my current situation, to succumb to the weight of my burdens and give in to despair.

But deep down, I knew that I couldn't continue down this path. I knew that I had to find a way to reclaim control of my life, to rediscover my sense of purpose and reignite the fire within me. And so, with renewed determination, I sought help from my church and counselling. I began to set out on a journey of self-discovery and healing, determined to emerge from the darkness stronger and more resilient than ever before.

The diagnosis I received did not define me; rather, it was the journey of resilience and redemption that ensued. With sheer determination and unwavering courage, and the invaluable support of several counselling sessions from my trauma therapist incorporating advanced neuroscience techniques, such as breath-work, Anti-saccades, saccades, and Eye Movement Desensitisation and Reprocessing (EMDR), I clawed my way back from the brink of darkness. Through these transformative experiences, I emerged stronger and more resilient than ever before.

Profound New Chapter in My Life

The counselling sessions, infused with advanced neuroscience techniques, marked the beginning of a profound new chapter in my life—a chapter defined by growth, healing, and transformation. As I delved deeper into the intricacies of these therapeutic modalities, I discovered a world of possibility—a world where perceived trauma could be altered, and peak performance could be redefined.

With each breath-work session, I found myself unraveling the layers of emotional distress that had weighed me down for so long. The rhythmic cadence of my breath became a powerful tool for grounding and centering, allowing me to release pent-up tension and connect with a sense of inner calm.

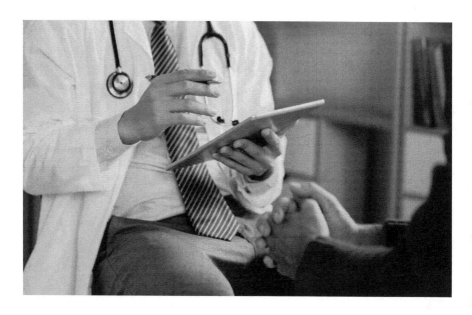

The "anti-saccades" and "saccades" therapy exercises challenged me to confront my subconscious patterns of thought and behaviour. Through these eye-movement exercises, I learned to redirect my attention away from negative stimuli and towards positive outcomes, rewiring my brain for resilience and adaptability.

And then there was EMDR—the groundbreaking therapy that revolutionised my approach to trauma healing. Through the use of bilateral stimulation, I was able to process and reframe traumatic memories, freeing myself from their grip and reclaiming control over my narrative.

With each counselling session, I felt myself growing stronger and more empowered. The wounds of the past began to heal, replaced by a newfound sense of hope and possibility. And as I integrated these transformative experiences into my daily life, I discovered a newfound capacity for peak performance.

No longer shackled by the chains of trauma, I embraced the challenge of redefining what it meant to perform at my best. Armed with a toolkit of advanced neuroscience techniques, I embarked on a journey of self-discovery and self-mastery, tapping into untapped reservoirs of potential and unlocking new levels of achievement.

As I reflect on this transformative journey, I am filled with gratitude for the counsellors and therapists who guided me along the way. In particular, Mr. Anson Yoo, the trauma therapist and counselor who later turned into a friend and a brother in Christ, supported me throughout this journey of recovery and helped me get back on track. His unwavering support and expertise provided the foundation upon which I built my path to healing and growth. As I step into this new chapter of my life, I do so with a renewed sense of purpose and possibility, knowing that the journey ahead is one of limitless potential and boundless opportunity.

In addition to individual therapy, my wife and I have also embarked on a journey of marriage counselling to improve our relationship and communication. It's an ongoing process that we recognise as necessary to strengthen our family unit and create a supportive, nurturing environment for ourselves and our children. Through open dialogue and a commitment to growth, we are laying the groundwork for a future filled with love, understanding, and resilience.

Navigating Life with Emotional Intelligence

With the insights gleaned from personal experiences, let's explore how we can navigate the intricate dance between work and personal life with emotional intelligence. We're all juggling different aspects of life—whether it's balancing career aspirations with family responsibilities, navigating the complexities of relationships, or managing financial pressures. These struggles often influence how we function on a day-to-day basis, shaping our responses and behaviours.

So, how can we cultivate emotional intelligence amidst life's myriad challenges? It begins with fostering self-awareness—a conscious effort to tune into our thoughts and emotions, acknowledging what is truly bothering us. One effective way to do this is by physically noting down our concerns, creating a tangible record that allows us to visualise and confront them head-on.

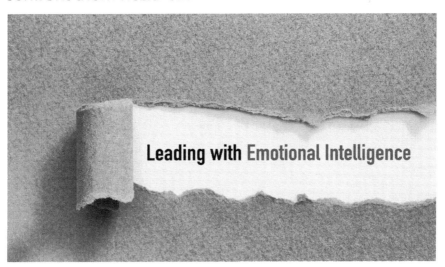

Once we've identified our sources of stress or discomfort, it's essential to assess how we're dealing with them. Are we simply allowing ourselves to be consumed by worry, or do we have actionable strategies in place to address these issues? Let's break it down into actionable points:

1. Identify Stressors:
Take a moment to list out the factors in your life that are causing you stress or discomfort. This could range from work-related deadlines to personal relationship challenges or financial worries.

2. Reflect on Your Responses:
Consider how you typically respond to these stressors. Are you prone to feeling overwhelmed and anxious, or do you tend to take proactive steps to address the underlying issues?

3. Develop Actionable Strategies:
Once you've identified your stressors and reflected on your responses, brainstorm actionable strategies to tackle them. This might involve breaking down larger problems into smaller, more manageable tasks, seeking support from loved ones or professionals, or implementing self-care practices to manage stress.

4. Track Your Progress:
Keep track of your efforts to address these stressors, noting any changes in your thoughts, emotions, or behaviours. Celebrate small victories along the way and be gentle with yourself during moments of difficulty.

By cultivating self-awareness, acknowledging our challenges, and taking proactive steps to address them, we can cultivate emotional resilience and navigate life's complexities with greater ease and grace.

The Role of Emotional Awareness and Neurological Responses

Delving into Daniel Goleman's seminal work, "Emotional Intelligence," we uncover the pivotal role of emotional awareness in navigating life's myriad challenges. Goleman's groundbreaking research underscores how self-awareness, self-regulation, and empathy form the bedrock of managing our emotional responses and achieving peak performance.

Self-Awareness:
At the heart of emotional intelligence lies the profound ability to understand our own emotional landscape. By peeling back the layers of our inner world, we gain insights into the intricate tapestry of our thoughts, feelings, and reactions.

Recognising our personal triggers and fears empowers us to anticipate and prepare for situations that might evoke negative emotional responses. Whether it's a looming deadline at work or a tense conversation with a loved one, self-awareness serves as our compass, guiding us through life's twists and turns with clarity and purpose.

Self-Regulation:
Armed with self-awareness, we embark on the journey of self-regulation—a process of mastering our emotional impulses and responses. In the face of adversity, stress, or conflict, the ability to maintain composure and resilience becomes paramount. Self-regulation entails developing a repertoire of strategies to cope with life's inevitable ups and downs. From mindfulness practices and deep breathing exercises to setting boundaries and practicing assertiveness, we cultivate a toolbox of skills to navigate the turbulent seas of our inner world. By harnessing the power of self-regulation, we ensure that our emotional state remains in harmony with our goals and aspirations, propelling us toward success and fulfilment.

Empathy:
Beyond the realm of self, empathy serves as a bridge connecting us to the emotions and experiences of others. As we extend our

awareness beyond ourselves, we cultivate a deeper understanding of the human condition—an understanding that transcends boundaries of race, gender, and culture. In the context of family dynamics and professional relationships, empathy becomes a cornerstone of effective communication and collaboration. By tuning into the perspectives and feelings of those around us, we foster a culture of trust, compassion, and mutual respect. Through acts of empathy, we not only mitigate conflicts and enhance teamwork but also forge deeper connections that enrich our personal and professional lives.

In essence, emotional awareness and neurological responses form the cornerstone of our journey toward self-mastery and interpersonal harmony. By cultivating self-awareness, mastering self-regulation, and embracing empathy, we unlock the door to a life of purpose, resilience, and profound connection.

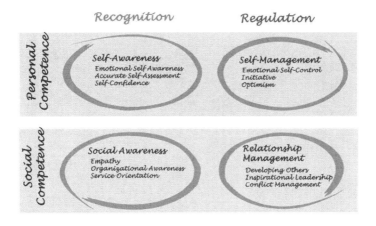

Three different mindfulness exercises that you can try:

Exercise 1

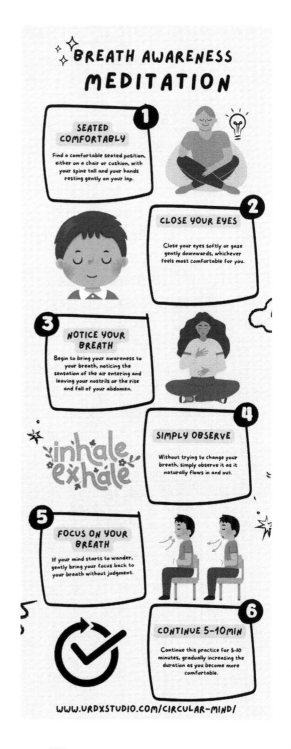

Exercise 2

Exercise 3
Mindful Walking

1. Find a quiet outdoor space where you can walk without distractions. It could be a park, garden, or even a quiet street.

2. Begin by standing still and taking a few deep breaths to ground yourself in the present moment.

3. As you start walking, pay attention to the sensations of each step—the feeling of your feet making contact with the ground, the movement of your legs, and the rhythm of your breath.

4. Notice the sights, sounds, and smells around you without getting caught up in them.

5. If your mind starts to wander, gently bring your focus back to the physical sensations of walking.

6. Aim to walk for 5-10 minutes, allowing yourself to fully immerse in the experience of mindful movement.

Chapter 9

"True leadership is not about standing at the top; it's about lifting others up and fostering meaningful connections on the journey to success."

Damian Tang

CHAPTER NINE

Leadership and Relationships: The Core of Success

Leadership is a multifaceted journey, deeply rooted in the quality of relationships forged along the way. My own leadership path has been richly defined by roles ranging from committee chairmanships to presidencies of prestigious landscape architecture associations, both domestically and on an international scale.

Each position has underscored a singular truth: the essence of leadership is not found in strategy or vision alone but in the power of relationships. This chapter explores the profound impact of relationship management on leadership success, integrating the cutting-edge insights of neuroscience with practical strategies for fostering trust, collaboration, and shared success.

Navigating the leadership landscape has revealed to me the indispensable value of building and nurturing relationships. In roles that demanded both a domestic focus and a global perspective, I discovered that successful leadership is inherently relational. Whether steering a committee, leading a national association, or guiding an international federation, the common denominator of success has always been the ability to connect, understand, and inspire people on a personal level. This journey has not only highlighted the importance of emotional intelligence but also the need for creating environments where trust and mutual respect can flourish.

Integrating Neuroscience into Leadership:

The exploration of leadership through the lens of neuroscience, particularly through the insights offered by Paul J. Zak's *The Neuroscience of Trust*, has been illuminating. Zak's research delves into how biochemical factors, especially oxytocin, influence trust-building and social bonding within professional environments.

These findings present a compelling case for leaders to consider the emotional and psychological well-being of their teams as central to organizational success. By fostering conditions that encourage the release of oxytocin, leaders can significantly enhance team cohesion, morale, and loyalty.

In this chapter, we're diving into how teams can work better together by understanding two important things: oxytocin and psychological safety.

First, let's talk about oxytocin. It's a hormone in our brains that helps us feel close to others. When we have more oxytocin, we tend to trust people more and feel connected to them. This hormone is like the glue that holds our relationships together. So, if we want our team to work well together, we need oxytocin to help us trust each other and feel connected.

But oxytocin isn't the only thing that matters. We also need something called psychological safety. This is all about creating an environment where everyone feels safe to share their ideas and take risks without worrying about being judged or criticised.

Imagine being on a team where everyone feels comfortable speaking up and sharing their thoughts. That's what psychological safety is all about. When people feel safe, they're more likely to be creative and come up with new ideas. And when teams have lots of different ideas to work with, they can come up with really innovative solutions to problems.

So, as leaders, it's important for us to create a team environment where everyone feels trusted and valued. By doing that, we can help our teams be more creative and successful.

Trigger Oxytocin within Our Teams

One way to trigger oxytocin to foster stronger bonds and trust among team members, is through acts of kindness and generosity. When team members show empathy towards each other, offer help without expecting anything in return, or express appreciation for each other's contributions, it can boost oxytocin levels. Something as simple as offering a listening ear or lending a helping hand can go a long way in building trust and camaraderie within the team.

Another way to stimulate oxytocin is through physical touch. While this might not be as applicable in all team settings, something as small as a pat on the back or a handshake can release oxytocin and reinforce feelings of connection. Even virtual teams can incorporate virtual high-fives or emojis to convey warmth and support, triggering oxytocin responses.

Shared experiences also play a crucial role in oxytocin release. When teams celebrate successes together, overcome challenges as a cohesive unit, or bond over shared interests and hobbies, it strengthens the sense of belonging and solidarity. Whether it's a team-building retreat, a collaborative project, or a shared meal, these experiences can trigger oxytocin and deepen the bonds within the team.

Furthermore, fostering a culture of trust and transparency within the team can sustainably elevate oxytocin levels. When team members feel safe to express their thoughts, share their vulnerabilities, and admit their mistakes without fear of judgment, it creates an environment where oxytocin can flourish. Leaders can lead by example by being open and honest in their communication, encouraging feedback, and demonstrating trust in their team members.

By incorporating these strategies into our team dynamics, we can create an oxytocin-rich environment where trust and connection thrive, paving the way for greater collaboration, innovation, and success.

Building Bridges Through Intentional Collaboration:

In our quest for expansion, it's imperative to navigate with clarity of purpose, seeking partnerships that resonate with our core values and objectives. By forging alliances rooted in a shared vision, we can transcend boundaries and unite diverse communities and stakeholders towards a common goal.

One potent strategy is to actively seek partnerships that align with our mission, values, and long-term objectives. By engaging with organisations, businesses, and individuals who share our passion and purpose, we can leverage collective strengths to drive meaningful impact and foster sustainable growth. Whether it's collaborating with like-minded nonprofits, aligning with socially responsible businesses, or partnering with community leaders, these alliances can amplify our reach and effectiveness in creating positive change.

Moreover, we can harness the power of networking platforms and industry events to facilitate meaningful connections and collaborations. By actively participating in relevant conferences, summits, and trade shows, we can engage with potential partners, clients, and stakeholders on a personal level. These platforms provide invaluable opportunities to showcase our expertise, share our vision, and forge genuine connections that lay the groundwork for fruitful partnerships. From networking sessions and panel discussions to interactive workshops and pitch competitions, these events offer a fertile ground for seeding new collaborations and expanding our network of allies.

Additionally, embracing digital networking tools and platforms can further enhance our outreach efforts and streamline the partnership-building process. From professional networking sites and online communities to virtual conferences and webinars, the digital landscape offers a myriad of opportunities to connect with diverse stakeholders from around the globe. By leveraging these digital platforms strategically, we can overcome geographical barriers, foster cross-sectoral collaborations, and tap into new markets and audiences with ease.

By embracing these strategies for expansion, rooted in clarity of purpose and a commitment to collaboration, we can forge powerful alliances, unite diverse communities, and catalyse positive change on a global scale.

Fostering Environments of Trust and Growth:

In the realm of leadership, trust stands as the bedrock upon which thriving teams are built. It's the invisible thread that weaves individuals together, fostering a sense of belonging, empowerment, and mutual respect. Creating an environment where genuine connections flourish isn't just a nicety—it's a strategic imperative for cultivating a motivated and high-performing team that can weather any storm.

Practical Approaches to Cultivating Trust:

1. Alignment of Actions and Words: Trust begins with authenticity. Leaders must ensure that their actions align with their words, embodying transparency and integrity in every interaction. By consistently demonstrating honesty, reliability, and ethical behaviour, leaders lay the foundation for trust to blossom within their teams. When team members witness this alignment between words and deeds, they feel reassured and inspired to reciprocate with their own trust and commitment.

2. Promotion of Transparency and Open Dialogue: Communication lies at the heart of trust-building. Leaders must create avenues for transparent dialogue, where team members feel encouraged to voice their thoughts, concerns, and ideas freely. This can be achieved through regular team meetings, one-on-one check-ins, and open-door policies that foster a culture of accessibility and approachability. By actively listening to their team members and valuing their input, leaders demonstrate respect and cultivate an atmosphere of psychological safety, where everyone feels heard and valued.

Practical Tools for Reinforcing Trust:

1. Transparent Project Management Tools: Utilising project management software that promotes transparency and accountability can enhance trust within teams. Platforms like Asana, Trello, or Monday.com provide visibility into project timelines, tasks, and responsibilities, allowing team members to track progress and collaborate effectively. By fostering transparency around project goals, milestones, and deadlines, these tools promote a shared understanding and alignment, reducing misunderstandings and fostering trust in the team's collective ability to deliver results.

2. Personal Connection Tools: In today's digital age, maintaining personal connections can be challenging, especially in remote or distributed teams. Leveraging tools like Slack, Microsoft Teams, or Zoom for virtual meetings and informal chats can help bridge the gap and reinforce personal connections among team members. Encouraging casual conversations, virtual coffee breaks, or team-building activities can foster camaraderie and strengthen interpersonal bonds, contributing to a culture of trust and collaboration.

Leaders can create environments where trust flourishes, enabling teams to unleash their full potential and achieve extraordinary results by implementing these practical approaches and leveraging appropriate tools. In nurturing a culture of transparency, open dialogue, and personal connection, leaders pave the way for growth, innovation, and collective success.

Leading with a Shared Vision: Inspiring Collective Purpose and Action

A shared vision serves as a beacon of inspiration, guiding teams towards a common destination and igniting a sense of purpose that transcends individual pursuits. It's the North Star that aligns diverse talents, energies, and aspirations, channeling them towards a unified goal and driving collective progress.

Implementing a Collective Vision:

1. Utilising Collaborative Platforms: In the digital age, collaborative platforms offer invaluable tools for developing and refining a shared vision that resonates with all team members. Whether it's a virtual whiteboard, project management software, or online brainstorming tool, these platforms provide a dynamic space for ideation, collaboration, and iteration. By leveraging the collective wisdom and creativity of the team, leaders can co-create a vision that reflects diverse perspectives and priorities, fostering a sense of ownership and commitment among all stakeholders.

2. Inclusive Visioning Process: To ensure alignment and ownership, it's essential to involve everyone in the visioning process. This means actively soliciting input and feedback from team members at all levels, regardless of their role or position. Whether through town hall meetings, focus groups, or online surveys, leaders can create opportunities for open dialogue and idea-sharing, empowering team members to contribute their insights, aspirations, and concerns. By co-creating the vision together, leaders cultivate a sense of shared ownership and investment in its success, fostering a deeper commitment and enthusiasm among team members.

3. Communicating and Reinforcing the Vision: Once the collective vision has been crafted, it's crucial to communicate it clearly and consistently to all stakeholders. This involves articulating the vision in simple, compelling language that resonates with the values and aspirations of the team. Whether through town hall meetings, email newsletters, or visual presentations, leaders must ensure that the vision is effectively communicated and reinforced across all channels. By continually reaffirming the shared purpose and direction, leaders inspire confidence and commitment, galvanising the team towards action and achievement.

Leaders can harness the power of shared purpose to mobilise teams to unlock their full potential, and achieve extraordinary results. In fostering a culture of collaboration, inclusivity, and shared ownership, leaders lay the foundation for sustained success and growth, driving meaningful impact and fulfilment for all.

Respecting Diversity and Fostering Inclusion: Nurturing a Culture of Belonging and Equity

In today's global landscape, diversity and inclusion are not merely ethical considerations but essential components of organizational success. Embracing diversity in all its forms—be it cultural, ethnic, gender, or cognitive—enriches the fabric of our teams and empowers us to harness the full spectrum of human potential. Inclusive environments not only foster innovation and creativity but also cultivate a sense of belonging and respect, where every individual can thrive and contribute their unique talents and perspectives.

Cultivating Inclusivity:

1. Engaging in Diversity Training: To cultivate a culture of inclusion, leaders must first invest in diversity training and education. This involves equipping team members with the awareness, knowledge, and skills needed to recognise and address biases, stereotypes, and systemic barriers that may impede inclusivity. By engaging in open and honest conversations about privilege, unconscious bias, and cultural competence, teams can cultivate empathy, understanding, and mutual respect. Creating spaces for sharing diverse experiences and perspectives further enriches the dialogue, fostering empathy and solidarity among team members.

2. Ensuring Every Voice is Heard and Valued: Inclusive leadership is about more than just representation; it's about creating an environment where every voice is heard, valued, and respected. Leaders must actively work to dismantle hierarchical structures and power dynamics that silence marginalised voices and perpetuate inequality. This involves creating opportunities for participation, collaboration, and decision-making at all levels of the organization. Whether through inclusive meeting practices, feedback mechanisms, or affinity groups, leaders must champion inclusivity by amplifying underrepresented voices and ensuring equitable access to resources and opportunities.

3. Recognizing the Strength in Diversity: Diversity is not just a checkbox—it's a strategic imperative that drives innovation, resilience, and growth. Leaders must actively celebrate and leverage the unique perspectives, experiences, and talents that diversity brings to the table. By fostering a culture of curiosity and openness, leaders can create an environment where differences are embraced as strengths rather than liabilities. This requires humility, empathy, and a willingness to challenge the status quo, as well as a commitment to continuous learning and improvement.

By embracing diversity and promoting inclusion, leaders not only fulfil their ethical duty but also unleash the complete capabilities of their teams. Through nurturing an atmosphere of inclusivity and fairness, leaders establish surroundings where individuals can excel, cooperate, and generate innovative ideas, thereby generating significant outcomes and long-lasting achievements.

Reflective Growth and Collective Development: Nurturing a Culture of Learning and Evolution

Let's talk about something that's near and dear to my heart: continuous learning and growth. You see, I believe that true leadership isn't just about knowing it all—it's about being willing to learn, adapt, and grow every step of the way.

So, how do we make sure we're always moving forward, both personally and as a team? Well, it starts with reflection. Taking the time to look back on our experiences, successes, and challenges can provide invaluable insights into where we've been and where we're headed.

That's why I'm a big advocate for journaling. Whether it's jotting down thoughts at the end of the day or keeping a gratitude journal, taking time for personal reflection can help us gain clarity, perspective, and self-awareness. And when it comes to team development, collective reflection is key. That's why I love organising team retreats—there's something powerful about stepping away from the day-to-day grind and coming together as a team to reflect, brainstorm, and set intentions for the future.

But reflection isn't just a one-time thing—it's an ongoing practice. That's why I'm always encouraging my team to engage in discussions about our progress towards our goals and areas where we can improve. Whether it's a casual check-in during a team meeting or a more structured performance review, creating space for open dialogue and feedback is crucial for fostering growth and development.

So, I invite you to commit to embracing reflective practices—both personally and collectively. By taking the time to pause, reflect, and learn from our experiences, we can continue to evolve, adapt, and thrive, both as individuals and as a team.

RECAP

Building Bridges Through Intentional Collaboration:

In today's interconnected world, leadership extends beyond individual achievement to encompass collective success. This paradigm shift necessitates an active intention to collaborate and expand network relationships.

Strategies for Expansion:
 - Seek partnerships with clarity of purpose, aiming to unite diverse communities and stakeholders.
 - Leverage networking platforms and industry events to facilitate these connections.

Fostering Environments of Trust and Growth:

Trust is the cornerstone of effective leadership. Creating an environment where genuine connections thrive is essential for a motivated and high-performing team.

Practical Approaches:
 - Ensure actions and words are aligned, promoting transparency and open dialogue.
 - Utilise tools for transparent project management and personal connection to reinforce trust.

Leading with a Shared Vision:

A shared vision is a powerful motivator. It transforms individual effort into collective action, amplifying the impact and satisfaction of the achievements.

Implementing a Collective Vision:
 - Use collaborative platforms to develop and refine a vision that resonates with all team members.
 - Involve everyone in the visioning process to ensure alignment and ownership.

Respecting Diversity and Fostering Inclusion:

Diversity and inclusion are not just moral imperatives but strategic assets. Balancing leadership voices with opportunities for all to be heard is critical for an inclusive environment.

Cultivating Inclusivity:
 - Engage in diversity training and create spaces for sharing diverse experiences and perspectives.
 - Actively work to ensure every voice is heard and valued, recognising the strength in diversity.

Reflective Growth and Collective Development:

Continuous learning and adaptation are hallmarks of effective leadership. Reflection on both personal growth and the development of stakeholders is crucial for identifying and bridging gaps.

Encouraging Reflective Practices:
- Support personal reflection through journaling and collective reflection through team retreats.
- Regularly engage in discussions on progress towards goals and areas for improvement.

The core of success in leadership is intricately linked to the strength and depth of relationships. By embracing both the science and art of relationship management, leaders can forge paths toward shared success, marked by trust, understanding, and genuine connection. This chapter serves as a testament to the transformative power of relational leadership, offering insights and strategies to inspire and guide leaders in their quest to build lasting bonds and achieve collective excellence.

Takeaways:

Transforming Leadership: Key Strategies for Impact

Modern leadership is about more than just giving orders; it's about genuinely connecting with your team and building trust. This section breaks down how leaders can overcome common challenges to make a real difference.

Moving Beyond Constant Activity:
- Being always busy can actually hurt the trust and confidence your team has in you. It might look like you're too focused on tasks and not enough on the people doing them.

- Simple Insight: Effective leadership is measured by the quality of your interactions with your team, not how packed your schedule is. Prioritise meaningful conversations and connections over a never-ending list of tasks.

Rethinking Leadership: Serve, Foster, and Communicate:
- Old-school leadership that's all about orders doesn't cut it anymore. Today's environment calls for leaders who can serve their team, foster growth, and communicate clearly.

- Simple Insight: Embrace a leadership style that focuses on supporting your team's development and ensuring everyone is clear on goals and expectations. This more inclusive approach not only boosts your leadership but also empowers your team to reach their full potential.

As we delve into these strategies, we see that leadership is a journey of growing together, celebrating achievements, and making lasting changes. By adopting these principles, you step into a leadership role that's all about building trust, encouraging development, and working together towards shared goals.

Leadership Language: Dos and Don'ts:

- Enhancing your leadership communication can significantly influence team dynamics, fostering an environment of trust, respect, and collaboration. Here's an expanded list of phrases to integrate or avoid in your daily interactions to cultivate a more empowering leadership style.

To Use:

1. "Let's work it out together" - Promotes teamwork and shared problem-solving.

2. "I value your input" - Demonstrates respect for team members' ideas.

3. "How can I support you?" - Offers help, emphasizing a servant leadership approach.

4. "Thank you for your hard work" - Acknowledges efforts and contributions.

5. "What are your thoughts?" - Invites open dialogue and diversity of thought.

6. "I trust your judgment" - Empowers team members, boosting their confidence.

To Use:

7. "Let's focus on solutions" - Encourages a constructive approach to challenges.

8. "I appreciate your dedication" - Recognizes commitment, enhancing morale.

9. "Your success is our success" - Highlights the importance of collective achievements.

10. "Can you help me understand?" - Shows willingness to listen and learn from others.

11. "This is what I'm thinking; what's your perspective?" - Shares ideas while valuing others' viewpoints.

12. "Let's celebrate our wins together" - Fosters a sense of community and shared joy in accomplishments.

Do Not Use:

1. "I'm too busy" - Suggests unavailability and can undermine trust.

2. "Just do it because I said so" - Discourages dialogue and undermines autonomy.

3. "That's not how we do things here" - Closes the door on innovation and new approaches.

4. "I don't need to know the details" - Implies disinterest in team members' work.

5. "It's not my problem" - Avoids responsibility, potentially damaging team cohesion.

6. "Figure it out on your own" - Signals a lack of support, leaving team members feeling isolated.

7. "I don't have time for this" - Indicates that team concerns are not a priority.

8. "We've always done it this way" - Resists change, possibly hindering progress.

9. "That won't work" - Immediately dismisses ideas without exploration.

Do Not Use:

10. "You should have known better" - Can be demeaning and doesn't contribute to learning.

11. "I expect no mistakes" - Sets unrealistic standards and can create a fear of failure.

12. "Don't bring me problems, bring me solutions" - While intended to encourage problem-solving, it can discourage team members from seeking guidance when needed.

Honestly, there have been times when I missed the mark. But I've learned to take a step back and reflect on how my words impact my team. It's not always easy to admit when I've fallen short, but I know that each interaction is an opportunity to learn and grow. If I realise that I haven't communicated effectively, I make a mental note to do better next time. It's all part of the journey of becoming a better leader and communicator.

By mindfully choosing phrases that encourage openness, respect, and collaboration, leaders can strengthen their relationships with team members, fostering a culture of mutual trust and shared success. Conversely, avoiding phrases that shut down conversation or imply disinterest can help prevent feelings of isolation or undervaluation within the team.

Chapter 10

"In the tapestry of a stress-free high achieving life, each principle is a thread; woven together, they create a masterpiece of productivity, leadership, and inner harmony."

Damian Tang

CHAPTER TEN

Integrating Purpose and Principles for a High Achieving Life

As we strive to become stress-free high achievers, it's essential to seamlessly integrate purpose and the principles we've explored into our daily routines. This chapter serves as a conduit between theory and practice, providing tangible steps to cultivate a harmonious balance between personal and professional growth. It's about translating our knowledge into actionable habits that prioritise sustainability and holistic well-being.

Begin with Purpose, End with Purpose: Navigating the Path to Stress-Free Achievement

In our quest to achieve excellence while maintaining our well-being, the journey begins and ends with purpose. It's not just about setting lofty goals or reaching milestones—it's about infusing every aspect of our lives with meaning and intentionality. This chapter serves as a guide, bridging the gap between theory and practice, to help us cultivate a seamless integration of key principles into our daily routines.

The principles we've explored hold the key to unlocking a balanced and fulfilling life. They are the compass that guides us towards our desired destination—a destination where success is not measured solely by external achievements, but by the alignment of our actions with our core values and aspirations.

But theory alone is not enough. We must translate our knowledge into actionable habits that promote sustainability and holistic well-being. It's about taking intentional steps to nurture our physical, mental, and emotional health, while also pursuing our professional goals with passion and purpose.

As we embark on this journey, let us remember that every action we take, every decision we make, should be rooted in purpose. Whether it's starting our day with a clear intention, practicing mindfulness to stay present and focused, or cultivating gratitude to foster a positive mindset, each small habit contributes to the larger tapestry of our lives.

So let us begin with purpose, and let us end with purpose. Let us strive to live each moment with intentionality and authenticity, knowing that true achievement is not found in the destination, but in the journey itself. Together, we can navigate the path to stress-free achievement and create lives that are both successful and deeply fulfilling.

Purposeful Integration: Guiding Principles for Daily Action

1. Commence with Self-Awareness

Start each day with a moment of introspection. Take a few quiet moments to tune into your thoughts, emotions, and physical sensations. This simple yet powerful exercise allows you to set a conscious intention for the day ahead, ensuring that your actions are aligned with your inner purpose and long-term goals.

2. Prioritise Tasks with Purpose Using the 2-Minute Rule

To navigate the demands of the day without feeling overwhelmed, apply the 2-minute rule: if a task requires less than two minutes to complete, tackle it immediately. This approach prevents small tasks from piling up and allows you to maintain a sense of organization and clarity throughout your day, enabling you to focus on what truly matters.

3. Time Blocking: Aligning Actions with Purpose

Allocate dedicated time blocks for various activities, both professional and personal. By structuring your day in this way, you can immerse yourself fully in complex tasks during focused work sessions while also ensuring that you carve out moments for relaxation and activities that bring you joy. This intentional approach to time management ensures that your daily actions are purpose-driven and aligned with your overarching goals.

4. Embrace Mindful Leadership: Leading with Purpose and Empathy

In your professional interactions, lead with mindfulness and empathy. Before responding in meetings or conversations, pause and take a deep breath, considering the most constructive and compassionate approach.

Mindful leadership cultivates a positive and harmonious work environment, fostering productivity, creativity, and collaboration—all driven by a shared sense of purpose.

5. Foster a Growth Mindset: Embracing Challenges as Opportunities

View challenges as opportunities for personal and professional growth, rather than obstacles to be overcome. Cultivating a growth mindset is essential for achieving success without succumbing to stress. Embrace a lifelong journey of learning and self-improvement, dedicating time to expand your knowledge and skills in areas that align with your purpose and aspirations.

6. Achieve Balance through Physical Activity and Rest

Integrate regular physical activity into your daily routine, choosing activities that you enjoy and can sustain over time. Equally important is prioritising restorative rest—ensure that you are getting enough sleep and incorporate relaxation techniques such as meditation or yoga into your schedule. By nurturing your physical well-being, you can maintain the energy and vitality needed to pursue your purpose with passion and resilience.

7. Reflect and Adjust: Nurturing a Culture of Continuous Improvement

End each day with a moment of reflection, acknowledging your successes and areas for growth. This practice fosters a mindset of continuous improvement, enabling you to refine your strategies and habits to better align with your purpose and aspirations. By embracing reflection and adjustment as integral parts of your daily routine, you can cultivate a life that is both purposeful and fulfilling, driven by a commitment to growth and authenticity.

Find Joy, Be Purpose-Driven

I find joy in every task I undertake, refusing to let stress dictate my pace. Each endeavour holds meaning and contributes to my purpose. Guided by my overarching goals, I navigate with purpose-driven tasks as milestones along the journey.

My personal journey toward integrating these principles began with a commitment to self-awareness. By starting each day assessing my mental, emotional, and physical state, I could tailor my activities and workload to align with my current capacity, leading to more sustainable productivity.

Implementing time blocks revolutionised my workday and personal time. Designating hours for deep work allowed me to tackle challenging projects without interruption, while setting aside
time for rest and hobbies helped maintain my well-being and creativity.

The shift to mindful leadership transformed my professional relationships. Now I respond to challenges with empathy and consideration, I nurtured a more collaborative and stress-free work environment, enhancing team productivity and satisfaction in my own business.

Quick Checklists for Mindful Integration

From the early chapters, we've learned several key principles for achieving a stress-free high achieving life. Here are a few checklists to help you integrate these principles into your daily routine:

Daily Self-Awareness Checklist
- [ ] Spend 5 minutes in silence assessing your state
- [ ] Set an intention for the day
- [ ] Identify your top three priorities

Time Management Checklist
- [ ] Apply the 2-minute rule for small tasks
- [ ] Schedule time blocks for work, rest, and play
- [ ] Limit distractions during deep work sessions

Well-Being Checklist
- [ ] Engage in at least 30 minutes of physical activity
- [ ] Practice mindfulness or meditation
- [ ] Ensure 7-9 hours of sleep

Professional Development Checklist
- [ ] Lead with empathy and consideration
- [ ] Embrace challenges as growth opportunities
- [ ] Reflect on the day's achievements and areas for improvement

Learning and Growth Checklist
- [ ] Dedicate at least 30 minutes to reading or learning a new skill
- [ ] Reflect on new learnings and how they can be applied
- [ ] Share insights or knowledge gained with others

Each step you take brings you closer to achieving a balanced, productive, and stress-free life. Remember, the goal is not perfection but progress towards integrating these practices into your daily routine for sustainable high achievement and inner harmony.

Conclusion

"As you embark on your path as a stress-free high achiever, remember: the destination is not a place, but a state of being; embrace the journey, and success will follow."

Damian Tang

CONCLUSION

Your Path Forward as a Stress-Free High Achiever

This conclusion aims to inspire readers to approach their personal and professional growth journeys with mindfulness, resilience, and strategic planning. By recognising the emotional phases of their journey and applying the suggested strategies, readers can better manage the inevitable ups and downs, leading to greater success and personal fulfilment.

Navigating the Emotional Journey of Growth

Every journey, especially those toward personal and professional growth, is paved with a mix of excitement, challenges, and revelations. Understanding the emotional landscape of this journey can equip you with the tools to navigate it successfully. Let's explore the phases of "Early Excitement," "Reality Check," and "The Big Challenge," and uncover strategies for managing emotions, willpower, and stress.

Early Excitement: The Spark Within

In the beginning, there's a spark—an idea or goal that ignites your passion and enthusiasm. This "Early Excitement" is characterised by boundless energy and a vision of what success looks like, often without a full understanding of the hurdles ahead. While this phase is essential for getting started, it's important to harness this energy wisely.

Strategy for Management: Ground your excitement with a plan. Set clear, achievable goals and break them down into actionable steps. This doesn't mean dampening your enthusiasm but channeling it into focused actions that move you forward, step by step.

Reality Check: Embracing the Journey

As you progress, you encounter the "Reality Check." This phase brings a deeper understanding of the complexities and challenges inherent in your path. It's a critical moment where your initial excitement might wane as the work becomes harder and the outcomes less certain. This reality check can be disheartening, but it's also a valuable opportunity for growth.

Strategy for Management: Cultivate resilience and adaptability. Recognise that challenges are not roadblocks but stepping stones. Engage in self-reflection to understand your reactions to setbacks and adjust your strategies accordingly. This is also the time to seek feedback and advice from mentors or peers who can provide perspective and guidance.

The Big Challenge: Finding Your Strength

"The Big Challenge" phase is where your resolve is tested the most. You may face significant obstacles that threaten to derail your progress. It's akin to facing the darkest part of the night just before the first light of dawn. Your energy reserves might be low, and your initial plans may need re-evaluation.

Strategy for Management: This is where managing your willpower, stress, and emotions becomes crucial. First, acknowledge your feelings without judgment. It's okay to feel overwhelmed. Next, focus on self-care to replenish your energy. This includes healthy eating, regular physical activity, and sufficient rest. Implementing mindfulness practices, such as meditation or deep-breathing exercises, can also help stabilize your emotions and reduce stress.

Remember, willpower is a finite resource. Prioritise tasks that align closely with your goals, and eliminate or delegate those that do not. Simplify your life and create routines that conserve your mental energy for the most critical decisions and tasks.

Moving Forward with Awareness and Strength

As you navigate through these phases, the key to sustained progress lies in self-awareness and the management of your emotional and physical well-being. Understand that the journey is not just about reaching a destination but about growing and learning along the way.

Embrace the early excitement, navigate the reality check with wisdom, and rise to the big challenges with resilience and courage. By doing so, you not only move closer to your goals but also become a more robust, more capable version of yourself.

Remember, every challenge you face and every obstacle you overcome adds to your story of success. The journey might be unpredictable, but with the right strategies and a mindful approach, you can navigate it with confidence and grace. The emotional journey of growth is a dynamic process that tests your resolve, strength, and adaptability.

Understanding the phases of this journey and employing strategies to manage emotions, willpower, and stress restored my strength. With resilience and awareness, you can navigate the path to success. During the writing of this book, I continued to improve and invest in myself. Little did I know, after weeks and months of investment training and learning, I would discover my capability as a value investor and begin thriving on wealth creation while maintaining my business and passion. Remember, challenges are not just obstacles but opportunities to learn, grow, and become stronger.

Living with Purpose: A Journey of Faith, Family, and Impact

As I conclude sharing my journey with you, I feel compelled to end with what drives me at the core: my purpose in life. For me, purpose isn't just a vague concept—it's a guiding light that illuminates every decision I make and every action I take.

As a firm believer in God, I see my purpose intertwined with His divine plan. I believe that I've been given certain talents and resources not just for my own benefit, but to do good for His people and the environment He has entrusted to our care. From my profession to the businesses I run, my overarching goal is always the same: to promote the well-being of both humanity and our planet. It's not just about making a profit; it's about making a difference.

This purpose also extends to the way I interact with others. I remind myself daily that every person I encounter is a beloved child of God, deserving of love, respect, and compassion. Whether it's my employees, customers, or strangers on the street, I strive to treat everyone with kindness and dignity, knowing that this is what God calls me to do.

But perhaps the most profound source of purpose in my life is my family—my wife and my daughter. They are my anchor, my motivation, and my greatest blessings. Knowing that they depend on me fills me with a sense of responsibility and determination unlike anything else. I am committed to being their protector, their provider, and their rock, no matter what challenges may come our way.

And when I look into the eyes of my daughter, I am reminded of the legacy I want to leave behind. I want her to grow up knowing that her daddy was not just a man who worked hard, but a man who made a difference in the world. I want her to be proud of the values I instilled in her, the example I set for her, and the impact I had on the lives of others.

So, as I share my story with you, I hope to inspire you to discover your own purpose and to live your life with intentionality and passion. Whether it's through your work, your relationships, or your daily actions, know that you have the power to make a difference in the world. And when you live with purpose, you not only enrich your own life, but you also leave a lasting impact on those around you.

I wish you all the best on this journey towards a stress-free, high-achieving life.

Your New Beginning

"Time is abundant in its essence, yet scarce in its passage; we possess plenty when honoured, but none when squandered in neglect."

Damian Tang

> *"For I know the plans I have for you,"* declares the Lord, *"plans to prosper you and not to harm you, plans to give you hope and a future."*
>
> Jeramiah 29:11 (NIV)

To download all the free resources from this book, kindly visit my website
www.urdxstudio.com/circular-mind/

urdxstudio@outlook.com

Made in the USA
Middletown, DE
14 August 2024

59082874R00102